*This special annotated edition is dedicated*
*in grateful recollection of his many kindnesses*
*to*

GEORGE SALIM ZAKHEM

*Philanthropist and ardent champion of*
*literary, artistic, and educational causes*

# *the* PROPHET

# Kahlil Gibran

*A* new annotated edition
introduced and edited by

SUHEIL BUSHRUI

ONEWORLD

# Contents

# INTRODUCTION

## Biography

Gibran Khalil Gibran was born in Bisharri, Lebanon on 6 January 1883. At the age of twelve he emigrated with his mother, half-brother and two younger sisters to the United States, where his first name was dropped and the spelling of 'Khalil' was changed to 'Kahlil' to suit American pronunciation. Once the family had settled in Boston, he returned to Lebanon for two years to study, and for a brief visit four years later in 1902, but otherwise never saw his native land again. Of the four members of his family in Boston, three fell untimely victims to tuberculosis; only Mariana, his first sister, survived beyond 1903 and would eventually outlive Kahlil himself.

While at school, Gibran developed a keen interest in literature and showed a flair for painting and drawing. At the age of twenty-two, his artistic talents were recognized by Fred Holland Day, a well-known Boston photographer, who organized an exhibition of his paintings. Another exhibition followed at the Cambridge School, whose owner and headmistress, Mary Haskell, subsequently became Gibran's confidante, patron and benefactor.*

Up to this point Gibran's writings had been little more than sketches, some of which provided material for later works. As yet

---

\* The relationship between Gibran and Mary Haskell is exceptionally well documented in two overlapping but by no means identical books (Hilu 1972 and Otto 1963). These two books are based on the correspondence between Kahlil Gibran and Mary Haskell, and Mary Haskell's memoirs as recorded in her journal.

not completely fluent in the English language, he began writing for an Arabic newspaper in Boston, and in 1905 his first book, *Al-Musiqah* (*Music*), was published. This was followed by *'Ara'is al-Muruj* (*Nymphs of the Valley*), in which he was fiercely critical of Church and State. He became known as something of a rebel, a reputation he confirmed with *Al-Arwah al-Mutamarridah* (*Spirits Rebellious*) in 1908.

The next two years were spent as a student at the Académie Julien and the Ecole des Beaux Arts in Paris, thanks to the generous sponsorship of Mary Haskell. In Paris he met the sculptor Auguste Rodin, who is said to have compared Gibran's work to that of William Blake – Gibran's fellow visionary in mode of thought, views on Church and State, grace of spirit and artistic style. Gibran's subsequent paintings and drawings contain many echoes of both Blake and Rodin, and Blake's influence pervades his writings.

Whilst in Paris he sketched portraits of a number of eminent people, including Rodin himself, the composer Claude Debussy, the actress Sarah Bernhardt and the poet W.B. Yeats. A particularly indelible impression was left on Gibran by another who sat for him while visiting the United States: 'Abdu'l-Bahá, son of the founder of the Bahá'í Faith. 'Abdu'l-Bahá's message celebrated the power and efficacy of an all-embracing unity. He emphasized the need to reconcile opposites, create harmony, and recognize the complementary values of each entity. It was this vision of unity in diversity that captured Gibran's thinking and philosophy. The influence of 'Abdu'l-Bahá on Gibran has been estimated in Susan Reynolds' interesting paper in which she states:

Alongside the influence of the writers and philosophers from whom Gibran drew insight and inspiration, there was another and equally significant one without which neither *The Prophet* (1923) nor *Jesus, the Son of Man* (1928) could have been written – certainly not in the form in which we now have them. It proceeded from yet another in the series of distinguished figures whom Gibran immortalized in a portrait, and perhaps the greatest of them all: 'Abdu'l-Bahá.*

Gibran said of 'Abdu'l-Bahá, 'For the first time I saw form noble enough to be a receptacle for the Holy Spirit';† and years later Gibran stated that 'Abdu'l-Bahá had provided a model for his *Jesus, the Son of Man*.‡ On his return to Boston, Gibran proposed marriage to Mary Haskell, who was ten years his senior. She declined the offer, but remained his lifelong friend and collaborator.

In 1912, Gibran moved to New York on the advice of his friend and fellow Lebanese émigré writer Ameen Rihani, and rented a studio which he called 'The Hermitage'. The same year saw the publication of his *Al-Ajninal al-Mutakassirah* (*The Broken Wings*), a semi-autobiographical tale of unrequited passion. *Dam'ah wa'lbtisamah* (*A Tear and a Smile*), a collection of prose poems, followed in 1914. Around this time Gibran began corresponding with May Ziadah, a young Lebanese writer living in Egypt, and over the next twenty years they formed a unique relationship, a love affair that took place entirely in their letters to one another, without their ever meeting.§

During the war years Gibran consolidated his knowledge of English, and by 1918 he was sufficiently fluent in the language of his adopted country to write and publish his first book in English. This was *The Madman*, a collection of Súfí-style parables. Two other Arabic works, *Al-Mawakib* (*The Procession*) and the powerful *Al-'Awasif* (*The Tempests*), as well as *Twenty Drawings*, a collection of his artwork with an introduction by Alice Raphael,

---

* Reynolds 2012. See also Bushrui and Jenkins 1998, pp. 9, 252–255.
† Honnol 1982, p. 158.
‡ Gail 1982, p. 228.
§ A number of Gibran's letters to May containing vivid and richly lyrical passages that rank alongside the best of his writing in Arabic have been published in a volume of English translations, *Gibran: Love Letters* (Bushrui and al-Kuzbari, 1995).

preceded the publication of his second book in English, *The Forerunner*, its form being similar to that of *The Madman*.

Soon afterwards Gibran and a group of fellow Arab émigré writers formed *Arrabitah* (the Pen Bond), a literary society that exerted a crucial shaping influence on the renaissance of Arabic literature in the United States. Among the founders was the distinguished Lebanese writer Mikhail Naimy, by now one of Gibran's closest friends.[*]

The yearning for *wahdat al-wudjud* (unity of being) – the Súfi concept with which *The Prophet* is infused – was encapsulated in Gibran's only play and last major Arabic work, *Iram Dhat al-'Imad* (*Iram, City of Lofty Pillars*). Published in 1921, it was a worthy precursor to *The Prophet* and incorporates many of the metaphors that Gibran was to use so successfully in the latter.[†] A smaller Arabic work, *Al-Badayi' wa'l-Tarayif* (*Beautiful and Rare Sayings*), followed in 1923, but this was completely overshadowed by the publication in the same year of his third book in English, *The Prophet*.

The success of *The Prophet* was unprecedented and won him universal recognition and acclaim; in America it outsold all other books in the twentieth century except the Bible, a major influence on its style and thought.

After the success of *The Prophet*, Gibran's health greatly deteriorated, but he managed to complete another four books in English: *Sand and Foam* (1926), *The Earth Gods* (1931), *The Wanderer* (published posthumously in 1932), and the finest of his late works, *Jesus, the Son of Man* (1928), a highly original collection of stories about Christ. Gibran died on 10 April 1931, at the age of just forty-eight, the cause of death being diagnosed

---

[*]  Naimy was one of Gibran's earliest biographers in Arabic and subsequently made his own translation of the book into English (see Naimy 1967). Though not factually reliable, it represents a fascinating insight into the mind and Arabian character of Gibran.

[†]  For further details of *Iram, City of Lofty Pillars*, its dealings with the Súfi concept of *wahdat al-wudjud* (unity of being) and its relationship to *The Prophet*, see Bushrui and Jenkins 1998, pp. 212–216.

as cirrhosis of the liver. His body was taken back to Lebanon and buried in a special tomb in Bisharri. An unfinished work called *The Garden of the Prophet*, which he intended as one of two sequels to *The Prophet*, was completed and published in 1933 by his companion and self-proclaimed disciple and publicist, Barbara Young.

## Writing *The Prophet*

By calling his second book in English *The Forerunner*, Gibran appears consciously to have designated it as the precursor of his most important work, *The Prophet*,* which followed it into print. The earlier book, published in 1920, certainly appears to anticipate *The Prophet* in the penultimate line of its final parable, 'The Last Watch', which predicts that 'out of our ashes a mightier love shall rise'. And Gibran himself affirmed that 'there is a sort of promise of *The Prophet* in the farewell of *The Forerunner*'.†

Exactly when Gibran first thought of the idea of *The Prophet* and when he started writing it have long been subjects of conjecture. According to Mary Haskell, he claimed to have in his possession 'the Arabic original of it, in elementary form, that I did when I was sixteen years old',‡ though no such original has ever been traced. In a letter to May Ziadah dated 9 November 1919, he attempted to explain how it evolved:

> As for *The Prophet* – this is a book which I thought of writing a thousand years ago, but I did not get any of its chapters down on paper until the end of last year. What can I tell you about this prophet? He is my rebirth and my first baptism, the only thought in me that will make me worthy to stand in the light of the sun. For this prophet had already 'written' me before I attempted to 'write' him,

---

*     Mikhail Naimy, 'A Strange Little Book', in Bushrui and Munro 1970, p. 90.
†     Hilu 1972, pp. 386–387.
‡     *Ibid.*, p. 322.

had created me before I created him, and had silently set me on a course to follow him for several thousand leagues before he appeared in front of me to dictate his wishes and inclinations.[*]

After its publication he wrote again to May:

This book is only a small part of what I have seen and of what I see every day, a small part only of the many things yearning for expression in the silent hearts of men and in their souls.[†]

There is no documentary evidence to show that Gibran worked on the book before June 1912, when, according to Mary Haskell, he 'got the first motif for his Island God' whose 'Prometheus exile shall be an Island one'.[‡] It therefore took at least eleven years to complete, during which time Gibran regularly broke off to write other works. All the while, however, he was rigorously refining and honing *The Prophet*, which was demonstrably closer to his heart than any of his other writings, and which he knew instinctively would be his finest work. He effectively completed it in 1922, but he was plagued with ill health and it was another year before it reached the printers.[§]

Gibran used Mary Haskell as a consultant on his English writings from the start, when he began writing *The Madman*. She tidied up the punctuation and grammar, and suggested alternative words for greater felicity of sound, on occasion. He looked upon her as a trusted and intelligent friend with a native command of his adopted language, and whose comments were therefore invaluable to him. Mary's testimony indicates that the literary collaboration started in June 1914,[¶] and thereafter he

---

[*]   Bushrui and al-Kuzbari 1995, p. 23.
[†]   *Ibid.*, p. 73.
[‡]   Hilu 1972, p. 90.
[§]   *Ibid.*, p. 401.
[¶]   *Ibid.*, pp. 193–195.

consulted her on the majority of the parables and poems in *The Madman* and *The Forerunner*, and on many of the sermons in *The Prophet*. The publication of the latter in 1923 marked the end of their collaboration.

Mary's journals contain several references to the 'Commonwealth'[*] and the 'Counsels'[†] as the Prophet was provisionally entitled in its early stages; earlier still, Gibran was also referring to it simply as 'My Book'.[‡] There were originally to be twenty-one 'Counsels' or sermons, but this was eventually expanded to twenty-six. In March 1918 he read to Mary what she called 'Passage to Men and Women', part of which she wrote down in her journal, and which would later be expanded into Almustafa's sermon on marriage:

> Love each other – and
> Let your love be as a sea between
> The shores of yourselves –
> Fill each other's cup – but drink not from
> One cup – Give bread to each other –
> But share not from the same loaf –
> Be each alone in your togetherness[§]

Gibran began sending Mary the 'Counsels' on which he was working, and she returned them annotated with helpful remarks,[¶] as well as greatly encouraging him with her appreciative response. In his letter of 11 June 1918 he wrote to her:

> In the 'Counsel' on houses the verb 'breed' was left out in copying. Of course it should read 'the holy spirit breed (or hide) in cells unvisited by sun and air'. And in that same 'Counsel' – how do you like 'and bees build not

---

[*]    Hilu 1973, pp. 312–313.
[†]    Hilu 1972, p. 303.
[‡]    *Ibid.*, p. 90.
[§]    Hilu 1973, p. 310.
[¶]    Hilu 1972, p. 309.

their hives on mountain peaks' in the place of 'butterflies flutter ... '?[*]

Gibran finally appears to have begun calling the book *The Prophet* in November 1919.[†] It was a crucial decision, as Mikhail Naimy observes:

> The very name 'Prophet' impresses with dignity and inspires reverence. A word said by a man clothed in prophetic majesty carries much more weight and magnitude than when said by a common man. Thus with that one word 'prophet' Gibran the artist raised to the dignity and height of prophecy what Gibran the poet had to say, even before he said it.[‡]

By May 1920, Gibran had plotted an overall scenario for *The Prophet*:

> In a city between the plains and the sea, where ships come in and where flocks graze in the fields behind the city, there wanders about the fields and somewhat among the people, a man – poet, seer, prophet – who loves them and whom they love – but there is an aloneness after all about him. They are glad to hear him talk, they feel in him a beauty and a sweetness; ... young women who are attracted by his gentleness do not quite venture to fall in love with him. And while the people count him as part of the city, and like it that he is there and that he talks with their children in the fields, there is a consciousness that this is all temporary – that someday he will go. And one day out of the blue horizon a ship comes towards the city and somehow everyone knows, though nothing is told,

*    Otto 1963, p. 579.
†    Hilu 1972, p. 322.
‡    Naimy 1967, p. 186.

that the ship is for the hermit poet. And now that they are going to lose him, the feeling of what he is in their life comes to them and they crowd down to the shore, and he stands and talks with them. And one says, 'Speak to us of Friendship' – and so on. And he speaks of these things. It is what he says about them that I have been writing. And when he has ended, he enters the ship and the ship sails into the mist.

And at the end one says to the poet, 'Tell us about God,' and he says, 'Of him have I been speaking in everything.' I am not trying to write poetry. I am trying to express thoughts. I want the rhythm and the words right so that they shan't be noticed but shall just sink in like water into cloth; and the thought be the thing that registers. But we must always remember too the man who is speaking. It is what that special personality says to the people he knows, and he has to speak in his own way.[*]

In September Gibran showed Mary the first draft of the prologue, and she wrote down as much as she could recall, some of which is very close to the final version:

Almustafa, the chosen and beloved, he who was a dawn unto his own day, had waited twelve years in the city of Orphalese, for the ship of purple sails to return and bear him back again to the isle of his birth.

Every day, upon the high hills without the city walls, he stood searching the distances for his ship. But the ship came not; and his heart grew heavy within him, for deep was the land of his memories and the dwelling-place of his greater desires. Then, in the twelfth year, on the seventh day of which is the month of awakening, came the ship of purple sails, and he descended the hills to go. But he could not go without pain, for all the self that he left in the city,

---

*    Otto 1963, p. 567.

and for his heart made sweet there with hunger and thirst. 'Fain would I take with me all that is here.' Yet, 'A voice cannot carry with it the tongue and the life that gave it wings. Alone it must seek the — and alone and without his nest shall the eagle fly across the sun.'

Now when he had descended from the hill, he turned again towards the sea and saw his ship approaching the harbour. And he beheld her mariners, the men of his own land, upon her bow ... he hails them, riders of the tides, and says, 'How often have you sailed in my dreams, and now you are come at this awakening, which is my deeper dream. Ready am I to go, and my eagerness, with sails full set, awaits the time ... But another breath will I breathe in this air then shall I go with you, a seafarer, among seafarers.

'And you, vast sea, sleepless mother, who alone are peace and freedom to the river and the stream, only another winding will this stream make, only another murmur in this glade, and then shall I come to you, a boundless drop to a boundless ocean.'

These things he said in words. But in his heart more remained unsaid. For he himself could not speak his deeper silence.

That much, Kahlil has written, and planned the rest. How Almustafa when he comes down from the hill whence he saw the ship, will find all the city meeting him, for now they know, and they know they love him; and they follow him, and ask him to counsel them, one after another questioning him; and to all of them he delivers his counsel; and then they go with him to the ship; and he speaks his farewell; and it is ended.*

A week later there was more:

---

* Hilu 1972, pp. 343–344. In Gibran's final text the word left blank in this section (Mary's memory presumably failing her for once) is 'ether'.

He brought the third writing on the setting for *The Prophet*. How, as he walked on, he saw afar the men and women leaving their fields and vineyards and hastening towards the gates of the city. And he heard many voices calling his name, and men shouting one to another from field to field telling of the return of his ship. And he said to himself: 'Shall the day of parting be the day of gathering and shall it be said that my eve was in truth my dawn? And what shall I give unto him who has left his plough in mid-furrow, and to him who has stopped the wheel of his winepress. Shall my heart be as a fruit-laden tree, that I may — and shall my desires become a fountain, that I may fill their cups? Am I a harp that the hand of the Mighty may touch me, and a flute that His breath may blow through me? A seeker of silences am I. And what treasures have I found in silences that I may dispense with confidence? If this is the day of my harvest, in what unknown fields have I sowed the seed, and in what unremembered seasons? If this be indeed the hour in which I shall lift up my lantern, it is not my own flame that shall burn therein. Empty and cold shall I raise my lantern, and the guardian of the night shall fill it with oil, and he shall light it also.' This he said in words. But more remained in his heart unsaid. For he himself could not speak his innermost silence.

And when he entered into the city, all the people came together to meet him and they cried unto him as with one voice. Then the elders of the city stood forth and said unto him, 'Go not yet away from us. A noontide have you been in our twilight, and your youth has given us dreams to dream. No stranger have you been among us, and not a guest, but our son and our beloved. Suffer not yet our hearts to hunger for your face.' And the priests and the priestesses said unto him, 'Let not the waves of the sea separate us now. You have walked among us, a spirit, and your shadow has been a light upon our faces. Let not the days you have passed in our midst become a memory that feeds upon the heart. Much have we loved you. But speechless was our love, and with veils has it been veiled. Now does it cry aloud unto you, and would be revealed before you. And ever has it been that love knows not its own depth until the day of separation.'

And many others came also and entreated him; and he answered not, but bent his head. And those who stood near him beheld his tears falling upon his breast.

'It was written down in a hurry,' said Kahlil. As we got to the text, we began at once to condense the connecting phrases. We always have a fine time over a manuscript, because one can talk to Kahlil as to one's self. There is no pride to guard, and no treasuring of phrases. He likes to work on and on and over and over until the thing is SAID. Sometimes we have to leave a thing to ripen in Kahlil. Never before has he written so systematically on an English book. So we are doing more than usual. Usually, he keeps things to show me, until he has completed them. But this Prophet prologue he brings in its first or second writing down. He says the final form comes quicker than when he prunes it alone. Our method is, first, Kahlil reads it through aloud to me. Then we look together at the text, and if we come to a bit that I question, we stop until the question is settled.

He knows more English than any of us, for he is conscious of the bony structure of the language, its solar system. And he creates English.

'I have been teaching myself to prune and to try for consciousness of structure. And this consciousness of structure is fundamental.'*

At this stage, Gibran appeared confident that the book would be published the following month, October 1920.† However,

---

* Hilu 1973, pp. 347–349. The phrase left incomplete by Mary became 'that I may gather and give unto them'.
† Hilu 1972, p. 250.

another year went by, and Almustafa's farewell was first heard by Mary in August 1921.[*] Still not satisfied that the book was complete, early in 1922 Gibran read her another sermon he had written, *On Pleasure*; together they 'changed a phrase or two for rhythm and closeness of fit'.[†] In May they worked on the 'final rhythmic forms' of *The Prophet* as well as the spacing,[‡] and he thought of another sermon, part of which was incorporated into the one on children:

> I think I'm going to write a 'Counsel' on receiving – everybody has something he wants to give – and so often no one will take. I may have a house and invite people to it. They will come and accept my house, my food, and my thoughts even, but not my love. And yet love is what most of us most want to give. People often say women want to be loved. But they really want much more. Many women want to bear children; and their very being wants to give children life. She often desires men just as a key to the child that is in her to give life to.[§]

After this, few changes or additions were made, and *The Prophet* finally went to press. Mary went over the galley proofs in April 1923, and of the corrections she made, Gibran wrote:

> Your blessed touch makes every page dear to me. The punctuations, the added spaces, the change of expressions in some places, the changing of 'Buts' to 'Ands' – all these things are just right. The one thing which I thought a great deal about, and could not see, was the rearrangement of paragraphs in Love, Marriage, Children, Giving and Clothes. I tried to reread them in

---

[*]    *Ibid.*, p. 362.
[†]    *Ibid.*, p. 368.
[‡]    *Ibid.*, pp. 381–384.
[§]    *Ibid.*, p. 386.

the new way, and somehow they seemed rather strange to my ear.[*]

At the end of September *The Prophet* was published. On receiving a copy, Mary was the first to recognize that its appeal would be universal. She was also aware that their association had now reached its climax. Coloured by emotion as her words were, Mary's ecstatic letter of 2 October 1923 nevertheless forecasts quite accurately the feelings of many among those millions who have been touched by the book since its publication:

> Beloved Kahlil, *The Prophet* came today, and it did more than realize my hopes. For it seemed in its compacted form to open further new doors of desire and imagination in me, and to create about itself the universe in nimbus, so that I read it as the centre of things. The format is excellent, and lets the ideas and the verse flow quite unhampered. The pictures make my heart jump when I see them. They are beautifully done. I like the book altogether in style.
>
> And the text is more beautiful, nearer, more revealing, more marvellous in conveying Reality and in sweetening consciousness – than ever. The English, the style, the wording, the music – is exquisite, Kahlil – just sheerly beautiful ... This book will be held as one of the treasures of English literature. And in our darkness we will open it to find ourselves again and the heaven and earth within ourselves. Generations will not exhaust it, but instead, generation after generation will find in the book what they would fain be – and it will be better loved as men grow riper and riper.
>
> It is the most loving book ever written. And it is because you are the greatest lover, who ever wrote.[†]

---

[*]    Otto 1963, pp. 644–645.

[†]    *Ibid.*, pp. 648–649.

Within a month all 1,300 copies of the first edition had been sold, setting in motion a trend that has continued inexorably up to the present day, and may perhaps be maintained for years to come. It represents a just reward and vindication for the American publisher Alfred Knopf, who was young and inexperienced when he took the bold gamble of publishing *The Madman* and all subsequent works in English by an unknown author.

There can be little doubt that in the case of *The Prophet*, Knopf followed Gibran's wishes to the letter, as the text concurs with those of Gibran's original manuscripts and typescripts that are available to us (these also contain several interesting corrections and deletions in his own hand, apparently made not long before publication, some of which are quoted among the annotations in these pages). The same integrity has characterized all of the many subsequent Knopf editions, which may therefore be regarded as definitive.

## Influences on *The Prophet*

A broad range of influences is detectable in *The Prophet*, including the Bible, Hinduism, Buddhism, Súfí mysticism, the Romantics, the popular schools of American thought, Ralph Waldo Emerson and William Blake with their respective beliefs in the Oversoul and the Universal Man, and Friedrich Nietzsche, whose Zarathustra resembles Gibran's own prophet in certain superficial respects but differs fundamentally in others. Gibran was also influenced by his friend Ameen Rihani, a fellow Lebanese expatriate writer for whose novel *The Book of Khalid* (1911) Gibran provided the illustrations.

## The Christian-Muslim synthesis

Gibran's identity as an Arab immigrant in America is central to any examination of his work, particularly his writings in English. However, no less important is the fact that he came from Lebanon, a country which perhaps more than any other has been a meeting point of East and West as well as a rich melting pot of religions, cultures and ideas. Although brought up a Maronite Christian, Gibran as an Arab was influenced not only by his own religion but also by Islam, and especially by the mysticism of the Súfís.

A firm believer in the teachings of the Gospels, Gibran found particular inspiration in the figure of Christ himself, eventually producing his own unique and powerful portrait of the Messiah in *Jesus, the Son of Man*, which was published three years before his death. Christ is also one of the models for Almustafa in *The Prophet*, and the form of the latter's teachings bears some comparison to the Sermon on the Mount in its eloquent guidance for humanity. Writing about Christ to Mary Haskell in 1909, Gibran declared, 'His life is the symbol of Humanity. He shall always be the supreme figure of all ages and in Him we shall always find mystery, passion, love, imagination, tragedy, beauty, romance and truth.'[*]

Whilst many of his opinions were modified over the years, this one remained constant throughout Gibran's life and was clearly with him when he wrote *The Prophet*. In 1921, Mary's journal has him describing Christ as 'the most powerful personality in history', who 'first perceived the Kingdom of Heaven in man's own heart, a world of beauty, of goodness, of reality, of truth'.[†] Similarly Gibran's depiction of the essence of Christ's teaching, again as recorded by Mary, is close to the central message of *The Prophet*: 'If the Kingdom of Heaven is within you, if you have that calm in yourself, that quiet in your center, if you are in love with life, you love your enemy because you love everybody'.[‡]

One of the most striking features of *The Prophet* is its biblical language, which Gibran rightly saw as the ideal medium for conveying profound precepts capable of being understood and digested. The part of the Bible that most appealed to him was

---

[*]    *Ibid.*, p. 27.
[†]    Hilu 1972, p. 359.
[‡]    *Ibid.*, p. 345.

the Book of Job, not least for the rhythm of its language.[*]
Shortly before *The Prophet* was published, Gibran told Mary,
'I know English only from Shakespeare and the Bible and you',[†]
and in July 1917 she wrote down his comments on the subject
of biblical language:

> The Bible is Syriac literature in English words. It is the child
> of a sort of marriage. There's nothing in any other tongue
> to correspond to the English Bible. And the Chaldo-Syriac
> is the most beautiful language that man has made – though
> it is no longer used.[‡]

There is virtually no part of *The Prophet* in which the language
of the King James Bible does not resonate – see especially the
Notes section on p. 76 for examples of occasions when this is
particularly evident. The Notes on pp. 70–71, on the other
hand, point out the influence of both the sayings of the Prophet
Muhammad and Súfí doctrine on the sermon *On Prayer*.

Gibran's attachment to Súfí philosophy finds its clearest
manifestation in his Arabic book *al-'Awasif* (*The Tempests*),
which contains short essays on three of the greatest figures
in Súfí literature: ibn-Sina (Avicenna), Ibnu'l Farid and
al-Ghazálí. Of Avicenna's poem 'A Compendium on the
Soul', Gibran writes, 'There is no poem written by ancient
poets nearer my own beliefs and my spiritual inclination'.[§] An
illustrious physician, mathematician and astronomer as well
as philosopher and poet, Avicenna inspires Gibran as one who
'reached the mystery of the soul by studying physical matter,
thus comprehending the unknown through the known'.[¶] By
contrast, the Arab mystical poet Ibnu'l Farid 'shut his eyes
against the world in order to see beyond it, and he closed his

---

[*] *Ibid.*, pp. 208, 384.
[†] Hilu 1973, p. 364.
[‡] *Ibid.*, p. 313.
[§] *Mirrors of the Soul* (Gibran 1965), p. 46.
[¶] *Ibid.*

ears against the tumult of the earth so that he could hear the eternal songs'.[*] And the ascetic philosopher al-Ghazálí, whose influence Gibran detected in Spinoza and Blake, 'searched for that hidden chalice in which the intelligence and experience of man is blended with his aspirations and his dreams'.[†] Gibran could almost have been describing his own Almustafa in these essays, which were written many years before *The Prophet* was published.

Gibran also wrote an Arabic poem entitled 'The Súfí', of which the following is an approximate translation:

> To God the praise be;
> Neither gold nor silver
> Have we.
> No movable
> And immovable property.
> Yoke-companion none.
> Nor offspring.
> And without lineage
> Through the earth
> Which stretches wide,
> As a phantom we traverse
> Whom no one can perceive
> Save in whose twin orbs
> The phantom hides.
> If we laugh,
> Distress lurks in time,
> And if we weep
> Behind it joy lies.
> We are but a spirit!
> Should you say to us:
> 'How wondrous!'
> Then forthright we reply:

---

[*]   *Ibid.*, p. 48,
[†]   *Ibid.*, pp. 49–50.

'By heaven!'
Wonder dwells
In your own
Veil of clay.[*]

The teachings of *The Prophet* correspond closely to the first level of Súfí teachings, which concern personal behaviour and the eternal and fundamental subjects central to life such as marriage, prayer, eating and drinking. And while the language and sentiment of *The Prophet* constantly remind one of the Bible and the English Romantics, the spirit and message is Súfí to its very core. The book is the sum of Gibran's Súfí thought and his social creed. It contains, in one form or another, all of the major Súfí ideas: the Universal Self, unity of life and death, unity of body and soul, unity of good and evil, unity of time and place, unity of religion, unity of humankind and collective responsibility, the divine in the human soul, and the relationship between essence and form. Both in this and in many of his other writings, Gibran makes reference to the Súfí ideal of the 'Greater Self', that is, God.

Above all, Almustafa is Christ and Muhammad merged into one, the embodiment of *al-Insan al-Kamil,* the 'Perfect Man' of Súfí tradition:

The Perfect Man is a miniature of Reality, he is the microcosm, in whom are reflected all the perfect attributes of the macrocosm. Just as the Reality of Muhammad was the creative principle of the Universe, so the Perfect Man was the cause of the Universe, being the epiphany of God's desire to be known; for only the Perfect Man knows God, loves God, and is loved by God.[†]

---

[*]     Orfalea and Elmusa, eds., 1988, pp. 34–35. The translation is by Andrew Ghareeb.
[†]     Arberry 1950, p. 101.

Hence Almustafa's words to the people of Orphalese: 'If aught I have said is truth, that truth shall reveal itself in a clearer voice, and in words more kin to your thoughts',[*] and 'I only speak to you in words of that which you yourselves know in thought'.[†]

This Eastern concept of the Perfect Man is paralleled in the West by that of the Universal Man and its variants, which include Emerson's Oversoul and perhaps even Nietzsche's Superman. Although derived from Jewish mysticism, the idea of the Universal Man – the universe as a single giant man composed of four elements – is most clearly expressed in the works of Swedenborg and, more especially, William Blake.[‡] The following (which could almost have been written by a Súfí) is from Blake's poem 'The Four Zoas':

> Four Mighty Ones are in every Man; a Perfect
> Unity
> Cannot Exist but for the Universal Brotherhood
> of Eden,
> The universal Man, to Whom be Glory
> Evermore. Amen.[§]

## Gibran and Blake

Although it is not entirely clear at what age Gibran first encountered the poetry and paintings of William Blake, there is no doubt that Blake had a profound impact upon him as a student in Paris in his mid-twenties. According to Mikhail Naimy, it was Auguste Rodin who awakened him to the subject; in 1909 Gibran attended a seminar in which the great French sculptor made extensive reference to Blake. 'I thought me a lonely wanderer; now is Blake with his torch lighting my path. What kinship is there between me and that man? Has his soul come back to this

---

[*]     *The Prophet*, p. 86.
[†]     *Ibid*., p. 88.
[‡]     *The Poems of William Blake* 1971, p. 288.
[§]     *The Complete Poetry & Prose of William Blake* 1988, p. 300.

earth to dwell in my body?"* Such (according to Mikhail Naimy) were the thoughts of the excited Gibran after hearing Rodin.

In a letter to Mary Haskell in 1915, a more mature Gibran wrote:

> Ruskin, Carlyle, and Browning are mere children in the kingdom of the Spirit. They all *talk* too much. Blake is the God-man. His drawings are so far the profoundest things done in English – and his vision, putting aside his drawings and poems, is the most godly.[†]

And three years later Mary herself expanded on this:

> Blake is mighty. The voice of God and the finger of God are in what he does ... He really feels closer to you, Kahlil, than all the rest, to me – and he feels more beyond and apart than all the rest, as if he moved in a larger consciousness.[‡]

By the time Gibran came to publish *The Madman* in 1918, his kinship with Blake and the meeting with Rodin had fused into the idea – improbable rather than impossible – that Rodin himself had compared Gibran to Blake. 'I know of no one else in whom drawing and poetry are so linked together as to make him a new Blake',[§] said the sculptor, according to Alice Raphael in her introduction to Gibran's *Twenty Drawings*. Other authors credit Rodin, or in some cases his associate Henri de Beaufort, with describing Gibran simply as 'the William Blake of the twentieth century'.[¶]

Gibran's American publisher Alfred Knopf not unnaturally chose the latter phrase to adorn the dust covers of *The Madman*,

---

*    Naimy 1967, p. 89.
†    Otto 1963, p. 444.
‡    Hilu 1972, p. 297.
§    Alice Raphael, 'On the Art of Kahlil Gibran', in Bushrui and Munro 1970, p. 127.
¶    For example, Anthony Ferris in Bushrui and Munro 1970, p. 127.

no doubt feeling that it mattered little whether either quotation was true. Whether apocryphal or not, they do serve to highlight the genuine affinity between Gibran and Blake. Indeed, detailed examination reveals that the influence of Blake upon Gibran's work was deeper and more enduring than that of any other individual writer or artist, Nietzsche included.

The most obvious attribute that Gibran shares with Blake is that they served twin muses. Both were poet-painters, perhaps even poet-prophets, in the sense of the poet as a revealer of eternal truths, the poet with the Messianic mission, the apocalyptic vision:

> Many convictions were common to both: a hatred of sham and binding orthodoxy, personified by evil priests; the manumission of physical love from the bonds of convention in order to attain spiritual completeness; the perception of beauty in the moment that seems to be fleeting but is, in truth, everlasting; and the discovery of miracles in seasonal nature and the commonplace things of daily living. Both warred against reason in the name of imagination. Both defied the snares of logic to cut a straight wingpath directly to God.
>
> To both Blake and Gibran these revelations are the gift of the poet. The Poet and the Prophet are one.[*]

Gibran, as has already been established, was heavily influenced by the Bible. No less is true of Blake who nevertheless – again like Gibran – reserved his strongest shafts of criticism for hypocrisy and corruption in the Church. Both men were social reformers, and both struggled to survive financially but maintained unswerving dedication to the work that was most important to them. Both also absorbed a rich variety of influences from contrasting sources, but had sufficient individualism and strength of character to knead these influences into a unique personal style

---

[*]    Robert Hillyer, 'Introduction to *A Tear and a Smile*', in Bushrui and Munro 1970, p. 177.

and message.[*] At a profound level, both poets sought to address the issue of how, in this fragmented existence, we can achieve the enlightenment and spiritual maturity that will enable us to reconcile the reality of life with the reality of the spirit.

For both poets, imagination, far from being the realm of the escapist, offered the key to divine reality, insight into the nature of things.[†] '"Imagination" is a way of knowing', Gibran is said to have remarked in 1912.[‡] For Blake, imagination is 'the Divine-Humanity'; it is the 'real & eternal World of which this Vegetable Universe is but a faint shadow, & in which we shall live in our Eternal or Imaginative bodies when these Vegetable Mortal bodies are no more'.[§]

Another characteristic common to both was a preoccupation with the depths of the psyche and so-called madness, from which they (unlike Nietzsche) fortunately remained immune, perhaps because their artwork provided a counterbalance for their poetry:

> Many poets ... have descended into the unconscious as far as Blake and Gibran, but they have not returned ... Blake and Gibran are two of the very few poets who have ventured that far and remained sane ... Blake returned, so did Gibran, fully sane, to report what they had seen.[¶]

Gibran's Almustafa is in some ways comparable to Los, the Prophet of Eternity in Blake's epic poems 'Milton' and 'Jerusalem'. Blake certainly identified with Los, as Gibran appears to have done with Almustafa:

> Like Almustafa, Los' great task is to turn the immortal eyes of man inward into the world of thought, into eternity

*     Cf. El-Hage 1980, p. 100.

†     *Ibid.*, p. 100.

‡     Hilu 1972, p. 85.

§     *The Complete Poetry & Prose of William Blake* 1988, p. 231.

¶     El-Hage 1980, p. 133.

ever expanding in the bosom of God ... Both prophets were revelers of the basic truth, spiritual revolutionists and the direct inspirers of the two poets.[*]

There are, equally, a number of important divergences between Gibran and Blake; no one could possibly suggest that one was a replica of the other. The principal difference lies in their respective views of nature. For Blake, nature is external and hostile, a projection of the fallen man: 'Where man is not, nature is barren.'[†] For his part, Gibran identifies with the Romantic view of the individual and nature, familiar to him through his reading of the New England Transcendentalists, especially Emerson, and of poets such as Coleridge and Wordsworth. 'I am trying to find myself through nature', he wrote to Mary Haskell from Paris in 1909. 'Nature is only the body, the form of God and God is what I seek and love to understand.'[‡] The Romantic vision of nature is very much in evidence in *The Prophet*, above all in the sermon *On Reason and Passion*, as discussed in the Notes section on p. 51. It is also worth mentioning at this juncture that Gibran's attitude to the natural world was a radical departure from its treatment in Arabic literature. In classical Arabic poetry, influenced by the desert way of life, nature was viewed as a force to be reckoned with; when the Arabs moved to the more fertile regions of the north and across North Africa to Spain, nature was treated as an ornament that was to be described as purely picturesque. Gibran, however, saw nature as invested with a life of its own with spiritual, emotional and intellectual dimensions; for him it was the link that binds us one to another, within it flowing a divine energy which is the perfect expression of the internal rhythm of all being. To commune with it was for Gibran akin to a religious experience. He regarded human life and the life of nature as complementary, sustaining each

---

[*]    *Ibid.*, p. 120.

[†]    *The Complete Poetry & Prose of William Blake* 1988, p. 38.

[‡]    Otto 1963, p. 31.

other in perfect symbiosis, which is the message of Shakespeare in *The Tempest.*[*]

Another major difference is that Gibran visualized the self evolving and eventually realizing the Greater Self though reincarnation, in which Blake did not believe. Nowhere in Blake's poetry can one find anything remotely like the following from Almustafa's farewell:

> A little while, and my longing shall gather dust
> and foam for another body.
> A little while, a moment of rest upon the wind,
> and another woman shall bear me.[†]

Nevertheless, the influence of and kinship with Blake is unmistakable in many of Gibran's works. For example, the title of one of his Arabic books translated into English, *A Tear and a Smile*, may well have been consciously derived from Blake's:

> What to others a trifle appears
> Fills me full of smiles or tears.[‡]

Books such as *The Madman* and *The Forerunner* display a Blakean sense of irony. And *Jesus, the Son of Man* bears the imprint of Blake's ideas about Christ, as has been demonstrated at some length by Kahlil Hawi and need not be reiterated here.[§]

---

[*] 'All things in this creation exist within you, and all things in you exist in creation; there is no border between you and the closest things, and there is no distance between you and the farthest things, and all things, from the lowest to the loftiest, from the smallest to the greatest, are within you as equal things. In one atom are found all the elements of the earth; in one motion of the mind are found the motions of all the laws of existence; in one drop of water are found the secrets of all the endless oceans; in one aspect of you are found all the aspects of existence.' *A Treasury of Kahlil Gibran* 1965, p. 140. See also Bushrui 1996, p. 38.

[†] *The Prophet*, p. 93.

[‡] *The Complete Poetry & Prose of William Blake* 1988, p. 721.

[§] Hawi 1963.

Blakean imagery and his use of the pathetic fallacy are frequently adopted by Gibran throughout *The Prophet*, as highlighted in further detail in the Notes sections.

In short, the benign shadow of William Blake is to be found virtually throughout all of the English writings of Gibran, as well as in many of his Arabic works. Moreover, there is perhaps no more compelling testimony to the influence of Blake upon Gibran than the latter's paintings and illustrations, especially those images which appear almost sculpted, as in the artwork of Blake.

## Gibran and Nietzsche

> Nietzsche he has loved since he was twelve or thirteen. 'His form always was soothing to me. But I thought his philosophy was terrible and all wrong ... Then by degrees I found more and more in Nietzsche. Gradually, I came to realize, that when we accept a man's form, we also accept his thought. For they are inseparable.'[*]

Despite this entry in Mary Haskell's journal, dated June 1912, there is no documentary evidence that Gibran had encountered any of the writings of Friedrich Nietzsche before going to Paris in 1908. In fact, it is quite likely that his discovery of Nietzsche more or less coincided with his discovery of Blake. But, as with the Gibran/Blake comparison attributed to Rodin, the accuracy or otherwise of Gibran's statement to Mary is relatively unimportant. What we know beyond doubt is that as a student he fell under the spell of *Thus Spake Zarathustra*, probably the only one of the German philosopher's works he ever read, and that while in Paris he wrote two articles in Arabic on Nietzsche.

In *Thus Spake Zarathustra*, written between 1883 and 1892, Nietzsche eulogizes the man who is free, titanic and powerful: the Superman. Claiming that 'God is dead', he repudiates

---

[*]    Hilu 1972, p. 88.

Christianity, especially its morality, arguing that the idea of the 'will to power' is central to human existence. The third concept explored in the book is that of 'eternal recurrence'. The linking framework is the story of the prophet Zarathustra, who expounds his philosophy in a series of 'discourses' on a wide variety of subjects, each ending with the words 'Thus spake Zarathustra'.

In all probability the ambiance of early twentieth-century Paris, dominated by whatever was considered fashionable, contributed in a large measure to Gibran's interest in Nietzsche. *Thus Spake Zarathustra* was all the rage and 'to have read Nietzsche meant to be modern'.[*] This was not merely modishness for its own sake; many of the leading poets of the day, including W.B. Yeats and T.S. Eliot, acknowledged Nietzsche's influence on them. For his part, the young Gibran was evidently drawn to Nietzsche, the iconoclast and critic of religion, at a time when he himself was inclined to attack corruption in the Church in works such as *Spirits Rebellious*. Perhaps, too, he perceived in Nietzsche 'the religious man underneath it all or in the philosopher's heart'.[†]

Writing in later years of their student days together in Paris, Yusef Huwayik recalled the misgivings he had had about his friend's newly acquired passion: 'Oh Gibran ... I am afraid that reading of Nietzsche has seduced you and influenced you. I do not like a frowning philosophy that ended in madness.'[‡] Gibran, however, was so dazzled that no one could have succeeded in deflating his enthusiasm, as demonstrated in a letter to another friend:

> Yes, Nietzsche is a great giant – and the more you read him the more you will love him. He is perhaps the greatest spirit in modern times, and his work will outlive many of the things which we consider great. Please, p-l-e-a-s-e, read

[*]   Stefan Wild, 'Nietzsche and Gibran', in Bushrui and Gotch 1975, p. 63.
[†]   *Ibid.*, p. 69.
[‡]   *Ibid.*, p. 64.

'Thus Spake Zarathustra' as soon as possible for it is – to me – one of the greatest works of all times.[*]

On his return to America, Gibran shared his discovery with Mary Haskell. 'Nietzsche to me is a sober Dionysus – a superman who lives in forest and fields – a mighty being who loves music and dancing and all joy', he wrote to her in May 1911.[†] As yet he was apparently untroubled by the German's obsession with self and denial of God; he went as far as to compare him with Christ, in a comment with obvious implications for Gibran's own *Jesus, the Son of Man*, written some fifteen years later with notable emphasis on the Nazarene's strength: 'Kahlil said Nietzsche was the occidental mind most like Christ's to him – that Nietzsche hated Christianity because it stood for softness.'[‡]

Together Gibran and Mary read and reread *Thus Spake Zarathustra*, albeit in an inferior translation,[§] but were nonetheless delighted by the author's 'exquisite wit or his boyish downrightness of phrase, so fresh'.[¶] In September 1912, according to Mary, Gibran was still in Nietzsche's thrall, describing him as 'probably the loneliest man of the nineteenth century and surely the greatest'.[**] However, by December of the same year, he 'disagrees with Nietzsche's conception of the returning cycle of identical experience. The return will always be in a different form.'[††]

From 1913 onwards, mention of Nietzsche all but disappears from the correspondence of Gibran and Mary Haskell and her journal. The clear inference is that Gibran was moving on. Whereas Blake remained, like an invisible companion,

[*]   Naimy 1967, p. 124.
[†]   Hilu 1972, p. 42.
[‡]   *Ibid.*, p. 86.
[§]   Stefan Wild, 'Nietzsche and Gibran', in Bushrui and Gotch 1975, p. 67.
[¶]   Hilu 1973, p. 88.
[**]  *Ibid.*, p. 97.
[††]  Otto 1963, p. 226.

Gibran's passion for Nietzsche abated and he began to see the philosopher's shortcomings in sharper relief. He had absorbed what he needed and what would be useful to him as a writer and thinker. Consequently, when it came to writing *The Prophet*, he was able to imitate the scenario of *Thus Spake Zarathustra* without in any way reproducing Nietzsche's philosophy. Gibran's prophet, like Zarathustra, sails back to his homeland after a long, self-imposed exile among a foreign people, and he gives them his wisdom in the form of sermons or discourses on a variety of topics. But he has none of Nietzsche's mordant intellect, his irony and his disenchantment. The need for compassion lies at the heart of Almustafa's teaching; to Zarathustra it represents weakness or self-indulgence. *The Prophet* is devoid of the Nietzschean echoes found, for example, in the first line of *The Forerunner*, 'You are your own forerunner'(directly derived from Zarathustra's 'Mine own forerunner I am'). Above all, Gibran's message, and the reassuring tone in which he delivers it, are worlds apart from that of Nietzsche.

However, the importance of Friedrich Nietzsche is perfectly encapsulated by Stefan Wild in his illuminating essay on the subject:

> Gibran admired Nietzsche in a fiery, emotional way. This, however, seems mainly true for the young Gibran. In later years and works Nietzsche becomes overshadowed by other literary figures such as Blake. In his early period Gibran moved sometimes close to Nietzschean nihilism. In later years we find only a formal affinity between Nietzsche's *Zarathustra* and Gibran's *Prophet*.[*]

To this may be added the following from Sarwat Okasha:

> When [Gibran] tried to wear the cloak of Nietzsche, it was but too evident that it was a borrowed garment. The

---

\*     Stefan Wild, 'Nietzsche and Gibran', in Bushrui and Gotch 1975, p. 74.

relationship between the two remained a relationship of dreams.[*]

## Gibran and Rihani

Ameen Rihani was one of the major pioneering forces who helped shape the renaissance in Arabic literature in the early twentieth century. Like Gibran, he was a Maronite Christian who migrated to the United States from his native Lebanon at the age of twelve. But whereas Gibran spent almost all his adult life in America, Rihani was constantly on the move between East and West, as befitted his role after the First World War as an Arab cultural ambassador and mediator.

Gibran and Rihani are said to have been childhood friends,[†] though their first documented meeting was towards the end of Gibran's student days in Paris.[‡] Gibran was immediately fascinated by the older man, seeing him as a kindred spirit, Rihani having already won considerable renown among Arab writers, especially in the West. Gibran no doubt looked to him as a model, describing him in one of his letters from Paris as 'a great poet',[§] though Rihani's lofty, sometimes rather academic style differed markedly from his own.

The year 1911 saw the publication in America of Rihani's novel *The Book of Khalid*, with illustrations by Gibran. Its influence on Gibran was substantial, not least in that it may well have encouraged and perhaps implanted in him the idea of writing in English himself.

Rihani's *The Book of Khalid* is a philosophical and largely autobiographical work employing an unusual narrative technique and somewhat florid language. It bears the unmistakable influence of Thomas Carlyle, who impressed Rihani greatly

---

[*]    Sarwat Okasha, 'Introduction to *The Prophet*', in Bushrui and Munro 1970, p. 152.
[†]    Hilu 1972, p. 39.
[‡]    Otto 1963, p. 46.
[§]    *Ibid.*

in his youth. The story of Khalid, the hero of Rihani's novel, begins in Baalbeck, his place of birth, where he becomes restless with the restricted way of life and decides to head for the land of material promise, America. He and his friend Shakib sell their mules and set off on a journey fraught with incident. In New York they find work as peddlers, hoping to work their way up to better-paid and less menial jobs. But while Shakib begins to prosper, Khalid continually struggles and becomes disillusioned about the New World, finding solace only in books about philosophy and metaphysics. After unhappy brushes with sex and politics, culminating in a ten-day jail sentence, he sets sail for his homeland with Shakib. Poignantly, he sums up his feelings of responsibility towards his compatriots: 'Our country is just beginning to speak, and I am her chosen voice. I feel that if I do not respond, if I do not come to her, she will be dumb for ever.'*

Back in his beloved Lebanon, however, Khalid is soon in trouble again. His lack of means prevents him from marrying his childhood sweetheart, and his attacks on the injustice of the Church result in excommunication and another jail sentence. After his release he spends some time in a hermitage on Mount Lebanon before making his way to Beirut and becoming the protégé of the wealthy Mrs Gotfry. Soon hailed as the prophet of the 'New Arab Empire', he is swiftly in trouble again for criticizing religious leaders and is forced to flee for his life. He returns to Baalbeck to find that his former sweetheart has been deserted by her husband. She and her baby travel with Khalid, Shakib and Mrs Gotfry to Cairo, where they enjoy brief happiness before the mother and baby perish and Mrs Gotfry departs. At the end of the book Khalid has disappeared without a trace, probably still dreaming of the unification of the human race, and of all things good.

Despite its flaws, particularly as a novel, *The Book of Khalid* is full of arresting and innovative ideas and its eponymous hero

---

*   Rihani 1911, p. 128.

is clearly a prophet figure almost as reviled as Christ himself. Whilst the form of the book was too complex and confusing for Gibran's own purposes, the idea of a sage dispensing wisdom among the people of a foreign land no doubt appealed to him. Although not as strong an influence as *Thus Spake Zarathustra*, Rihani's book may be said to have foreshadowed *The Prophet* in that it conveys the teachings of the East in the language of the West, and was written by an Arab who appreciated the best of both worlds. It remained only for Gibran to find the right medium and words to express the message at the heart of his – and Rihani's – philosophy: that of love, beauty and reconciliation.

## *The Prophet:* message, form and style

*The Prophet* clearly evolved over a number of years, perhaps even for as long as two decades between Gibran's adolescence and the mature period of his writings. He was not prepared to finalize it until he felt sure it would be nothing less than perfect. Gibran was awaiting his moment.

The moment came, perhaps not surprisingly, in the wake of the First World War, a shattering experience even for those not directly involved. Gibran finally began to piece together the fragments of inspiration that had come to him, adding to them, developing and moulding them into the final form of *The Prophet*. He was now ready to make his definitive statement. In February 1918, as the war was drawing to a close, he wrote to Mary Haskell:

> Human beings have changed remarkably during the past three years. They are hungry for beauty, for truth, and for that other thing which lies beneath and beyond beauty and truth.[*]

---

[*]    Hilu 1972, p. 299.

In retrospect, these words can be seen as the foundation for what was shortly to flow from Gibran's pen. The results came four years later; as the work was nearing completion he summed up his view of his latest book: 'The whole *Prophet* is saying just one thing: "You are far, far greater than you know – and All is well"'.* In the words of the thirteenth-century mystic Ibn al-'Arabi:

> How do you deem yourself but a meagre planet
> When locked within you is the whole universe?

*The Prophet* occupies a unique place in world literature, which makes assessment of its true value a difficult task for the critic. Often unjustly branded as a romanticized version of universal philosophical and religious teachings, it has in some ways been a victim of its own astonishing success. The reality is that it is a work of remarkable compassion, insight, hope and inspiration, with a timeless message that combines the dignity of the Christian Bible and the wisdom of the Súfís of Islam, phrased with a simplicity and rhythmical quality that renders it accessible to a wide readership. Mikhail Naimy, who saw much of it being written, offers an eloquent explanation for its success:

> It is not the skeleton ... that sets *The Prophet* apart; it is the spirit and vision that animates it, that makes it breathe with the reactions of an impassioned, high-strung and over-sensitive soul that had known the full range of human experiences from extreme dejection to the highest exaltation. It is too the music that cascades in words; the colours that make dead letters dance in rhythmic abandon; the shafts of light that pierce the darkness as lightning pierces the clouds. It is, finally, the gates of a heart flung open to the world that it may see

---

* Hilu 1973, p. 360.

what miracles the magic hand of suffering had wrought in it. It is all that and more that makes *The Prophet* Gibran's masterpiece.[*]

Gibran's own testimony indicates that he found the inspiration for the work's spellbinding language and cadences in nature:

> Poets ought to listen to the rhythm of the sea. That's the rhythm of Job – and in all the magnificent parts of the Old Testament. You hear it in that double way of saying a thing, that the Hebrews used. – It is said – then said right off again – a little differently. And that's like the waves of the sea. You know how a big wave rolls in – whish! – and carries the big pebbles with it in a crashing noise. Then some of the pebbles roll back again, with a smaller noise, a sort of undercurrent of sound – and then a second wave will roll up, smaller than the first – whish! – And then there's a pause. – And soon another big wave will come – and the same thing happens all over again.
>
> That's the music to learn from – and the music of the wind – and the rustle of the leaves.[†]

The above offers some explanation as to why this little book of teachings comes across to the reader as a far less didactic work than, for example, *Thus Spake Zarathustra*. *The Prophet* owes its broad appeal partly to the clarity, universality and timelessness of its message, and partly to the power of its poetry. On its publication, the Irish mystic Æ (George Russell) wrote:

> I do not think the East has spoken with so beautiful a voice since the *Gitanjuli* of Rabindranath Tagore as in *The Prophet* of Kahlil Gibran ... I could quote from every

---

[*]   Mikhail Naimy, 'A Strange Little Book', in Bushrui and Munro 1970, p. 91.
[†]   Hilu 1972, p. 384.

page, and from every page I could find some beautiful and liberating thought.[*]

Many years later, Mikhail Naimy reflected that:

> One will not do justice to a book like *The Prophet* if one is to take it as a book of instructions only. Its greater value ... lies in the mould in which those instructions are cast. Because he was a consummate artist, Gibran was able to make his Almustafa sing sweet melodies and paint exquisite pictures as he expounded his views of human life to the people of Orphalese. Those songs and those pictures have something intoxicating in them. Never before or after had Gibran attained that mastery of sound and colour ... Such books and such men are our surety that Humanity, despite the fearful dissipation of its incalculable energies and resources, is not yet bankrupt.[†]

*The Prophet* is among the most consoling and least cynical literary works of a century often characterized as the Age of Anxiety. It represents an appeal for a return to and reconciliation with nature, emphasizing the relationship that binds individuals to their environment and fellow creatures. They all become denizens of one world bound together by life and death. Those who err are not alone, and those who reach the sublime heights share the glory with all; our destiny lies in the way we act towards one another, and the salvation of the individual is the salvation of society. Thus Almustafa sets out his own version of the golden rule common to all great religions: that we must do as we would be done by. What he voices is not some unattainable ideal but practical wisdom and simple moral and spiritual values, laced with a strong sense of Súfi destiny: for everything there is a time, as in sunrise and sunset, ebb and flow.

---

[*]   George Russell (Æ), 'Kahlil Gibran', in Bushrui and Munro 1970, p. 91.
[†]   Mikhail Naimy, 'Gibran at His Peak', in Bushrui and Gotch 1975, p. 9.

Like all great poets, Gibran endeavours to show how opposites can be reconciled: good and evil are inseparable; joy and sorrow are one because each feeds on the other, as do body and soul; life and death are a source of each other; we have neither past nor future – 'Yesterday is but today's memory, and tomorrow is today's dream.'[*] The poet himself is representative of this reconciliation at all levels:

> For Gibran, the East and the West, the pagan and the Christian, the ancient and the modern, the past and the present, came together to reaffirm his faith in the 'Unity of Being'; and the image of the eternal re-birth of beauty and passion in [the secular figure of] Adonis joined forces with the message of Christ, who taught selfless love, so that this in turn confirmed him in his passionate belief in the healing power of Universal Love.[†]

The great driving force behind Gibran's most poignant outpourings of compassion and love in *The Prophet* was not passion for any one individual, profound though his feelings were for both Mary Haskell and May Ziadah in their different ways; rather it was his intense yearning for fulfilment in the form of oneness with life and with his work, oneness with God, a yearning constantly fuelled by his earthly situation:

> To be an emigrant is to be an alien. But to be an emigrant mystical poet is to be thrice alienated. To the geographical alienation is added the estrangement from both conventional human society at large ... and also the whole world of spatio-temporal existence. Therefore such a poet is gripped with a triple longing: a longing for the country of his birth, for a utopic human society of the imagination in which he feels at home, and for a higher

---

[*]    *The Prophet*, p. 63.

[†]    S.B. Bushrui, 'Gibran and the Cedars', in Bushrui and Gotch 1975, p. 27.

world of metaphysical truth. This triple longing provided
Gibran with the basis for his artistic creativity.[*]

## 'Yearning' and the Súfí idea of journeying

> Every man ... according to Gibran, is a longing: the longing
> of the divine in man for man the divine whom he had
> previously been ... every man is destined for Godhead. Like
> the seed, he bears within him the longing, the fulfilment
> which is God, and the road leading to this fulfilment.[†]

The keynote of *The Prophet*, as in much of the work of the
Romantic poets, is pantheism. Its central article of belief is
that God is latent within everyone as a Greater Self, and that
this is attained through aspiration, or 'yearning', which is
comparable to prayer in religion, and also through successive
reincarnations. Life is a journey, and God is both starting point
and destination. 'Like a procession you walk together towards
your god-self,' says Almustafa in the sermon on good and evil,[‡]
whilst the Qur'án (v:18) tells us that 'Allah's is the Sovereignty
of the heavens and the earth and all that is between them, and
unto him is the journeying'.[§] The journey thus represents the
condition of full awareness when the soul has embarked on the
path leading to its desired union with God. The enlightened
wayfarer (Almustafa is one of the names given to the Prophet
Muhammad) offers directions for anyone who would undertake
such a journey:

> Almustafa can ... symbolize the man who ... has become
> his freer self; who has realized the passage in himself

---

[*]    Nadeem Naimy, 'Kahlil Gibran: His Poetry and Thought', in Bushrui
and Gotch 1975, pp. 35–36. Nadeem Naimy is Mikhail Naimy's nephew.

[†]    *Ibid.*, p. 46.

[‡]    *The Prophet*, p. 41.

[§]    Pickthall (undated), p. 98.

from the human to the divine, and is therefore ripe for emancipation and reunion with life absolute ... The people of Orphalese ... stand for human society at large in which men, exiled in their spatio-temporal existence from their true selves, that is from God, are in need in their Godward journey of the guiding prophetic hand that would lead them from what is human in them to the divine. Having made that journey himself, Almustafa poses in his sermons throughout the book as that guide. [*]

Thus Almustafa, like Krishna in the *Bhagavadgita*, reincarnates not only out of the need for continued self-realization, but also to provide an example and guidance for the spiritually uninitiated.

The idea of 'journeying' to God was developed by the great Súfí poet-philosopher Ibn al-'Arabi into the theory that understanding of oneself and knowledge of the cosmos is attained by travelling through it. For him, all creation was symbolized by a gigantic circle: the individual journeys from any point on the circumference along an abundant choice of paths or radii towards the centre, where he or she merges with the Divine Presence or the Absolute. The principal way is through self-purification by heeding God's solemn covenant and by following the example of the Perfect Man or 'Prophet'. [†]

The three types of journey, according to Ibn al-'Arabi, are away from God, towards God, and in God. A journey away from God could be one with a purpose such as reward or punishment, the journey of a fallen angel or one turning away in shame or disobedience, or a mission to humankind. Such journeys are dangerous unless carried out under the direction of the Almighty, as are journeys towards God, of which the classic types are undertaken by those who do not worship one god or who think He is not the sole Creator; or, alternatively, it is an

---

[*]   Nadeem Naimy, 'Kahlil Gibran: His Poetry and Thought', in Bushrui and Gotch 1975, p. 47.
[†]   Ibish 1977–1978, pp. 206–207.

impeccable, God-guided journey. Examples of journeys in God, carrying no rewards but still dangerous, are the rational journey of philosophers and others likely to lose their way without a guide, or the journey of prophets or apostles.[*] This concept, although purely Súfí in origin, no doubt greatly appealed to Gibran on account of its universality:

> Implicit in Ibn al-'Arabi's theory of journeying is the unity of religions. To him revelation is universal and every prophet has transmitted an aspect of God's Will to humankind. Therefore, if we examine the inner contents of all religions by journeying inwardly from the external forms towards the inner one we will find a transcendent unity: they all emanate from the same supreme Center.[†]

The essence within the diversity of forms is the love of God, as Almustafa teaches. And the journey is an inner one, a spiritual one, in contrast to the travels of the twenty-first-century man or woman, which are all physical.[‡] Hence the timelessness of *The Prophet*'s message. The spiritual journey is analogous, as Mikhail Naimy points out, to Gibran's own career up to the publication of his finest work in 1923:

> *The Prophet* represents the peak in his literary career. Viewed in the light of Reincarnation, a doctrine which he embraced and made the cornerstone of his philosophy of human destiny, Gibran's life from his own birth to the birth of *The Prophet* may be seen as a steady ascent to that peak.[§]

\*     *Ibid.*, pp. 209–210.
†     *Ibid.*, pp. 210–211.
‡     *Ibid.*, p. 211.
§     Mikhail Naimy, 'Gibran at His Peak', in Bushrui and Gotch 1975, pp. 3–4.

# Gibran's symbols in *The Prophet*

'I am the maker of symbols', Gibran is said to have remarked to his friend and fellow student in Paris, Yusef Huwayik,[*] and although evidently derived from a variety of sources, Gibran's symbolism was his own. Like the prophets of the Old Testament and Christ himself, Gibran often explained his symbols, and was fond of using forms such as the apophthegm and the parable, always with a moral. But he never attempted to bamboozle his readers, nor did he use symbols for their own sake, but rather to convey a simple message as powerfully as possible. Talking of the sermon on freedom, he remarked to Mary Haskell:

> I want to say only those things that are at the source of things. I want the root out of which the fruits will grow. I want to use figures and symbols that are planetary. I use the footprints as a figure, because the footprint will be here as long as there is a planet.[†]

On the same theme, he continued:

> 'Almustafa' in Arabic means something special, the Chosen and the Beloved, too, really between them both ... All that is written here is written with many things in mind. Each thing is a symbol of a man's life as a whole, and the 'land of his memories' is all our historic past. Life bears us from our great past towards our future.[‡]

The following are the principal symbols employed by Gibran in *The Prophet*, some of them near universal in their application, others intensely personal:

---

[*]   Huwayik 1976, p. 19.
[†]   Hilu 1972, p. 340.
[‡]   *Ibid.*, p. 344.

| | |
|---:|:---|
| *dawn* | the source of knowledge |
| *sea* | the Great Spirit or Greater Self |
| *ether* | Freedom |
| *a boundless drop to a boundless ocean* | the Self yearning to return to its source |
| *tree, fountain* | fertility and giving |
| *lantern* | the Self full of awareness and receptive to inspiration |
| *houses* | enslaving traditions |
| *larger body* | nature, the forest, the world of freedom |
| *children of space* | those freed from the shackles of materialism |
| *songs and silences of night* | Inspiration |
| *clothes* | (attachment to) obsolete traditions |
| *sun and wind* | liberty, freedom |
| *north wind* | the power of enslaving traditions |
| *god-self, giant-self* | the Almighty towards whom all souls yearn |
| *well-spring* | eventful life of mysteries unceasing and unfathomable |
| *the ear of one's ear* | Insight |
| *temple invisible* | the temple of the soul |
| *veil* | mind, ignorance and unknowing |
| *greater silence* | Death |
| *mist* | mystery and eternity |
| *giant oak tree covered with apple blossoms* | God |
| *hills* | the dimensions of thought and inspiration |
| *crystal* | Clarity |
| *dream* | life of earth |
| *tower in the sky* | hope for a future of spiritual fulfilment |

## Gibran's illustrations

Several outstanding examples of Gibran's artwork are to be found among the drawings he used to illustrate his own writings, especially *The Prophet*, and also in the only book devoted entirely to his artwork, *Twenty Drawings*. The latter was published in 1919 with a foreword by the leading art critic of the day, Alice Raphael. Though somewhat hyperbolic in tone, Raphael's essay, one of the earliest to highlight the affinity between Gibran and William Blake, succeeds to the extent of capturing the essential quality of Gibran the artist:

> It is at [the] dividing line of East and West, of the symbolist and the ideationist, that the work of Kahlil Gibran presents itself as an arresting type in our conception of painting ... we see a body of a woman who rises out of the vast form of the All-Mother, carrying in her arms man and woman ... Erda – Amida – Ceres – Mary – the choice is a matter of time and temperament. The meaning is the same and Gibran is dealing with fundamentals ... He senses the meaning of the earth and her productions; of man, the final and the consummate flower, and throughout his work he expresses the interrelating unity of man with nature ... His centaurs and horses have a charm beyond their natures so that they are never wholly animal in character ... in regarding these centaurs we sense the beast that is yet man and again the man which is and must be animal; we become conscious of that evolution upward which is in itself a miracle, although there is a barrier which will forever prevent man from clutching the stars.[*]

This same quality, albeit on a scale befitting the medium, is to be found in Gibran's illustrations. The illustrator's art is in many ways analogous to that of the piano accompanist, whose aim is neither to outshine nor to be submerged but to complement

---

[*]   Alice Raphael, 'On the Art of Kahlil Gibran', in Bushrui and Munro 1970, pp. 133, 135–136.

the soloist. Gibran's illustrative work generally harmonizes so well with his poetry that it is hard to conceive of one without the other.

Arguably no illustration by Gibran surpasses the twelve to be found in *The Prophet*, particularly the frontispiece depicting the face of Almustafa. This and the last illustration in the book, the 'Creative Hand', were originally done in black and white, the other ten being wash drawings. An apt and penetrating description of these illustrations has been provided by Mikhail Naimy:

> Taken as a whole Almustafa's face is, perhaps, the loveliest and the most impressive ever drawn by Gibran, not excluding that of Jesus done a few years later. The large, dreamy eyes seem to look away beyond the present moment and the immediate circumstance. Sorrowful and penetrating, they speak eloquently of a most sympathetic heart and a soul suffused with loving understanding. The mouth, though thick-lipped and passionate, is rich in sensitiveness, patience, forgiveness and delicacy of taste. It is the mouth of one who has tasted the pleasures of the world and found them bitter, and would no longer soil his lips with a drop from that fountain. The effect of that delicate veil of sadness drawn all over the face is broken by the barely suggested circle of hair forming a halo of light. Framed within that halo are eternities of painful struggle against all the things that keep man chained to the earth and make of his life a tug of war between good and evil, birth and death. Though the struggle be yet going on, and the wounds it caused be yet bleeding, the issue is not in doubt.

> The 'Creative Hand' represents an outstretched hand, sensitive, powerful, graceful, beautifully sculpted, and with an open eye in the middle of it that seems to see all things. Around the eye is a cyclone-like whirl of wings. Around the whirling wings is a dark abyss heaving with chaotic

shadows and fringed with a chain of human bodies. That is the hand of God. It sees as it touches, and imagines as it sees. It imagines forms before it creates them; then touches chaos and out of it makes all forms to issue as by magic. In drawing that hand Gibran's memory may have carried him back to the hand of God by Rodin. The two may have something in common in so far only as the basic idea of creation is concerned; but they are vastly different in conception and execution.

The rest of the drawings in the book are either interpretive of some thoughts, or represent new thoughts not expressed in words; but are all deeply symbolic and very delicately executed, the delicacy in some cases being almost tantamount to effeminacy. Though lacking in the touch of masculinity, those drawings, without exception, bespeak the grandeur of the imagination that conceived them and the wonderful sensitiveness of the hand that gave them form. An example of that is the drawing of 'Pain'. It represents a woman crucified on the chests of two men whom she loves equally and by whom she is equally loved. Neither can she divide her heart between the two, nor would either of the two be content with less than her whole heart. What greater pain can there be than the pain of love becoming a cross to the lover? On the other hand, what joy can be greater than the joy of Love leading to the cross, and from the pains of the cross to the bliss and emancipation of Love triumphant?[*]

---

\*    Naimy 1967, pp. 191–193.

# THE PROPHET

*The twelve illustrations in this volume are reproduced
from original drawings by the author*

# The Coming of the Ship

Almustafa, the chosen and the beloved, who was a
dawn unto his own day, had waited twelve years in
the city of Orphalese for a ship that was to return
and bear him back to the isle of his birth.

And in the twelfth year, on the seventh day of Ielool,
the month of reaping, he climbed the hill without
the city walls and looked seaward; and he beheld
his ship coming with the mist.

Then the gates of his heart were flung open, and his
joy flew far over the sea. And he closed his eyes
and prayed in the silences of his soul.

But as he descended the hill, a sadness came upon
him, and he thought in his heart:

How shall I go in peace and without sorrow? Nay, not
without a wound in the spirit shall I leave this city.

Long were the days of pain I have spent within its
walls, and long were the nights of aloneness; and
who can depart from his pain and his aloneness
without regret?

Too many fragments of the spirit have I scattered in
these streets, and too many are the children of my
longing that walk naked among these hills, and
I cannot withdraw from them without a burden
and an ache.

It is not a garment I cast off this day, but a skin that I
tear with my own hands.

Nor is it a thought that I leave behind me, but a heart
made sweet with hunger and with thirst.

Yet I cannot tarry longer.

The sea that calls all things unto her calls me, and I must embark.

For to stay, though the hours burn in the night, is to freeze and crystallize and be bound in a mould.

Fain would I take with me all that is here. But how shall I?

A voice cannot carry the tongue and the lips that gave it wings. Alone it must seek the ether.

And alone and without his nest shall the eagle fly across the sun.

Now when he reached the foot of the hill, he turned again towards the sea, and he saw his ship approaching the harbour, and upon her prow the mariners, the men of his own land.

And his soul cried out to them, and he said:

Sons of my ancient mother, you riders of the tides,

How often have you sailed on my dreams. And now you come in my awakening, which is my deeper dream.

Ready am I to go, and my eagerness with sails full set awaits the wind.

Only another breath will I breathe in this still air, only another loving look cast backward,

And then I shall stand among you, a seafarer among seafarers.

And you, vast sea, sleepless mother,

Who alone are peace and freedom to the river and the stream,

Only another winding will this stream make, only another murmur in this glade,

And then shall I come to you, a boundless drop to a boundless ocean.

And as he walked he saw from afar men and women
     leaving their fields and their vineyards and
     hastening towards the city gates.
And he heard their voices calling his name, and
     shouting from field to field telling one another of
     the coming of his ship.

And he said to himself:
Shall the day of parting be the day of gathering?
And shall it be said that my eve was in truth my
     dawn?
And what shall I give unto him who has left his plough
     in midfurrow, or to him who has stopped the
     wheel of his winepress?
Shall my heart become a tree heavy-laden with fruit
     that I may gather and give unto them?
And shall my desires flow like a fountain that I may fill
     their cups?
Am I a harp that the hand of the mighty may touch
     me, or a flute that his breath may pass through
     me?
A seeker of silences am I, and what treasure have
     I found in silences that I may dispense with
     confidence?
If this is my day of harvest, in what fields have I sowed
     the seed, and in what unremembered seasons?
If this indeed be the hour in which I lift up my lantern,
     it is not my flame that shall burn therein.
Empty and dark shall I raise my lantern,
And the guardian of the night shall fill it with oil and
     he shall light it also.

These things he said in words. But much in his heart
     remained unsaid. For he himself could not speak
     his deeper secret.

And when he entered into the city all the people came
    to meet him, and they were crying out to him as
    with one voice.
And the elders of the city stood forth and said:
Go not yet away from us.
A noontide have you been in our twilight, and your
    youth has given us dreams to dream.
No stranger are you among us, nor a guest, but our
    son and our dearly beloved.
Suffer not yet our eyes to hunger for your face.

And the priests and the priestesses said unto him:
Let not the waves of the sea separate us now, and
    the years you have spent in our midst become a
    memory.
You have walked among us like a spirit, and your
    shadow has been a light upon our faces.
Much have we loved you. But speechless was our love,
    and with veils has it been veiled.
Yet now it cries aloud unto you, and would stand
    revealed before you.
And ever has it been that love knows not its own depth
    until the hour of separation.

And others came also and entreated him. But he
    answered them not. He only bent his head; and
    those who stood near saw tears falling upon his
    breast.
And he and the people proceeded towards the great
    square before the temple.

And there came out of the sanctuary a woman whose
    name was Almitra. And she was a seeress.
And he looked upon her with exceeding tenderness,
    for it was she who had first sought and believed in
    him when he had been but a day in their city.

And she hailed him, saying:

Prophet of God, in quest of the uttermost, long have
    you searched the distances for your ship.

And now your ship has come, and you must needs go.

Deep is your longing for the land of your memories
    and the dwelling place of your greater desires;
    and our love would not bind you nor our needs
    hold you.

Yet we ask ere you leave us, that you speak to us and
    give us of your truth.

And we will give it unto our children, and they unto
    their children, and it shall not perish.

In your aloneness you have watched with our days,
    and in your wakefulness you have listened to the
    weeping and the laughter of your sleep.

Now therefore disclose us to ourselves, and tell us all
    that has been shown you of that which is between
    birth and death.

And he answered,

People of Orphalese, of what can I speak save of that
    which is even now moving within your souls?

'Almustafa' heralds the central figure of *The Prophet* as a man of inner
purity; in addition to its standard meaning of 'the chosen one', the word
is derived from the Arabic *safa* which is regarded by some scholars as the
basis for the term 'Súfí'. The name Almustafa implies the possession of
spiritual knowledge and divine characteristics and also represents the
Western concept of the Universal Man as well as the concept of *al-Insan
al-Kamil*/the Perfect Man.

Many of the symbols employed by Gibran throughout *The Prophet*
(see p. li for an extended list) occur in this introductory passage,
such as the mention of the sea – the Great Spirit or the Greater Self,

'ether' – freedom, 'a boundless drop to a boundless ocean' – the Self yearning to return to its source, 'tree ... fountain' – fertility and giving. The 'lantern' is the self that is full of awareness and therefore receptive to inspiration. One of the most universal of symbols, the lantern or lamp represents – among other things – life, immortality, the light of divinity, wisdom, the intellect, guidance, transitory individual existence, good works and remembrance.

The reference to dawn – the source of knowledge – in the second line is also crucial. In Christianity, the dawn symbolizes the resurrection and the advent of the Messiah bringing light into the world and thus introduces Almustafa as a comparable individual; indeed, he shares many characteristics with the figure of Christ that Gibran was later to portray in *Jesus, the Son of Man*. Although it is tempting to see Almustafa as a personification of Kahlil Gibran himself in his compassion for humanity and great wisdom, Gibran was keen to stress that he did not consider himself to be this pure being; as discussed in the biography *Kahlil Gibran: Man and Poet*, Gibran several times declared to Mary Haskell when working with her that 'this is not I, but The Prophet'.[*] Furthermore, Naimy confirmed that Gibran never once intended to 'parade before men in a prophetic mantle'.[†] Similarly, critics have commonly made rather too facile an equation of Orphalese with America. Almitra has likewise been taken as Mary Haskell and the 'isle of his birth' as Lebanon, but the latter rather signifies the unborn state, while Naimy suggests 'the bosom of the All-Spirit, or the centre of Life Universal'.[‡]

'Ielool' is September, the month of mellowness, the beginning of autumn, which symbolizes maturity, ripeness, culmination, the end of one cycle and the beginning of another. It is interesting to note that if one compares the published edition with the images of the original manuscript as in William Shehadi's *Kahlil Gibran: a Prophet in the Making*,[§] Gibran substituted this for the original 'Nissan' – the month of April and beginning of spring. It seems thus that Gibran wished to emphasize the harvest of Almustafa's wisdom and experience in the autumn of his life; similarly, it suggests a desire to place as much focus on reflecting on what we can learn from this life as on the dawning of our immortality and place with God.

---

[*]   Bushrui and Jenkins 1998, p. 212.
[†]   Naimy 1967, p. 193.
[‡]   *Ibid.*, p. 189.
[§]   Shehadi 1991, p. 159.

# On Love

Then said Almitra, Speak to us of Love,
And he raised his head and looked upon the people,
    and there fell a stillness upon them. And with a
    great voice he said:
When love beckons to you, follow him,
Though his ways are hard and steep.
And when his wings enfold you yield to him,
Though the sword hidden among his pinions may
    wound you.
And when he speaks to you believe in him,
Though his voice may shatter your dreams as the
    north wind lays waste the garden.

For even as love crowns you so shall he crucify you.
Even as he is for your growth so is he for your
    pruning.
Even as he ascends to your height and caresses your
    tenderest branches that quiver in the sun,
So shall he descend to your roots and shake them in
    their clinging to the earth.

Like sheaves of corn he gathers you unto himself.
He threshes you to make you naked.
He sifts you to free you from your husks.
He grinds you to whiteness.
He kneads you until you are pliant;
And then he assigns you to his sacred fire, that you
    may become sacred bread for God's sacred feast.

All these things shall love do unto you that you may
    know the secrets of your heart, and in that
    knowledge become a fragment of Life's heart.

But if in your fear you would seek only love's peace
    and love's pleasure,
Then it is better for you that you cover your
    nakedness and pass out of love's threshing-floor,
Into the seasonless world where you shall laugh, but
    not all of your laughter, and weep, but not all of
    your tears.

Love gives naught but itself and takes naught but
    from itself.
Love possesses not nor would it be possessed;
For love is sufficient unto love.

When you love you should not say, 'God is in my
    heart,' but rather, 'I am in the heart of God.'
And think not you can direct the course of love, for
    love, if it finds you worthy, directs your course.

Love has no desire but to fulfil itself.
But if you love and must needs have desires, let these
    be your desires:
To melt and be like a running brook that sings its
    melody to the night.
To know the pain of too much tenderness.
To be wounded by your own understanding of love;
And to bleed willingly and joyfully.
To wake at dawn with a winged heart and give
    thanks for another day of loving;
To rest at the noon hour and mediate love's ecstasy;
To return home at eventide with gratitude;
And then to sleep with a prayer for the beloved in
    your heart and a song of praise upon your lips.

In exhorting the people of Orphalese to embrace all aspects of love, Almustafa acknowledges the pain that is as much to be valued and accepted as the pleasure of it; love must be welcomed in all its parts to be experienced fully. As Gibran wrote in *The Voice of the Master*, 'love passes us by, robed in meekness; but we flee from her in fear, or hide in the darkness; or else pursue her, to do evil in her name'.[*] Love is to be accepted as it comes. In the same way, Gibran wrote as follows to May Ziadah in February 1924:

> Do not fear love, friend of my heart. We must surrender to it in spite of what it may bring in the way of pain, of desolation, of longing, and in spite of all the perplexity and bewilderment.[†]

The concept of love as wounding and painful – even while it can uplift to ecstasy – is found in the writings of both the Súfís and the medieval Christian mystics.[‡]

The phrases 'God is in my heart' and 'I am in the heart of God' may be compared to the Islamic tradition 'neither my earth nor my heaven contains me, but I am contained in the heart of my servant who believes'. Other fruitful comparisons for this sermon are to be found in Blake's poem 'The Clod and the Pebble':

> 'Love seeketh not itself to please,
> Nor for itself hath any care,
> But for another gives its ease,
> And builds a heaven in hell's despair.'

> So sung a little Clod of Clay,
> Trodden with the cattle's feet,
> But a Pebble of the brook
> Warbled out these metres meet:

---

[*]   *The Voice of the Master* (Gibran 1958), p. 46.
[†]   Bushrui and al-Kuzbari 1995, p. 82.
[‡]   See Bushrui 1989, p. 70 for further discussion.

'Love seeketh only Self to please,
To bind another to its delight,
Joys in another's loss of ease,
And builds a hell in heaven's despite.'

We are also reminded of 1 Corinthians 13:4–8:

Charity suffereth long, and is kind; charity envieth not; charity vaunteth not itself, is not puffed up,

Doth not behave itself unseemly, seeketh not her own, is not easily provoked, thinketh no evil;

Rejoiceth not in iniquity, but rejoiceth in the truth;

Beareth all things, believeth all things, hopeth all things, endureth all things.

Charity never faileth: but whether there be prophecies, they shall fail; whether there be tongues, they shall cease; whether there be knowledge, it shall vanish away.[*]

---

[*]    *The Holy Bible*, King James Version.

# On Marriage

Then Almitra spoke again and said, And what of
    Marriage, master?
And he answered saying:
You were born together, and together you shall be
    forevermore.
You shall be together when the white wings of death
    scatter your days.
Ay, you shall be together even in the silent memory of
    God.
But let there be spaces in your togetherness,
And let the winds of heaven dance between you.

Love one another, but make not a bond of love:
Let it rather be a moving sea between the shores of
    your souls.
Fill each other's cup but drink not from one cup.
Give one another of your bread but eat not from the
    same loaf.
Sing and dance together and be joyous, but let each
    one of you be alone,
Even as the strings of a lute are alone though they
    quiver with the same music.

Give your hearts, but not into each other's keeping.
For only the hand of Life can contain your hearts.
And stand together yet not too near together:
For the pillars of the temple stand apart,
And the oak tree and the cypress grow not in each
    other's shadow.

15

With its successful blending of both practical advice centred on a strong, loving understanding of human nature and allusion to eternal, preordained mystical union, it is not surprising that this text is an extremely popular choice for wedding-ceremony readings. Mary Haskell quoted Gibran in May 1923:

> Marriage doesn't give one any rights in another person except such rights as that person gives – nor any freedom except the freedom which that person gives.[*]

Similarly, Gibran stated his views on marriage in an interview with the *Evening Sun* newspaper printed on 28 December 1914:

> [Marriage] is the attraction of complement and supplement, invariably the coming together of two great natures for whom there is no other choice but marriage, from which eternal recreating is the only result.[†]

It is fascinating to note that the words Gibran chooses to describe marriage in *The Voice of the Master* echo his profound longing for the unity of religions in his depiction of two souls coming together in wedlock:

> It is the higher unity which fuses the separate unities within the two spirits.[‡]

---

[*]    Hilu 1972, p. 404.
[†]    Bushrui and Jenkins 1998, pp. 148–149.
[‡]    *The Voice of the Master* (Gibran, 1958), p. 150.

# On Children

And a woman who held a babe against her bosom
said, Speak to us of Children.
And he said:
Your children are not your children.
They are the sons and daughters of Life's longing for
itself.
They come through you but not from you,
And though they are with you yet they belong not to
you.

You may give them your love but not your thoughts,
For they have their own thoughts.
You may house their bodies but not their souls,
For their souls dwell in the house of tomorrow, which
you cannot visit, not even in your dreams.
You may strive to be like them, but seek not to make
them like you.
For life goes not backwards nor tarries with
yesterday.
You are the bows from which your children as living
arrows are sent forth.
The archer sees the mark upon the path of the
infinite, and He bends you with His might that
His arrows may go swift and far.
Let your bending in the archer's hand be for
gladness;
For even as He loves the arrow that flies, so He loves
also the bow that is stable.

Despite never having any of his own, Gibran found a sense of joy and freedom in the company of children, their innocence and purity of heart enriching his own awareness. A particularly delightful vignette tells of a summer spent in Scituate (south of Boston) where he befriended the local children for whom he made kites. Claiming to have made sixty or seventy for them, they were soon making kites of their own too and after judging a parade of the best of them, Gibran presented the winner with his own best one. He later announced to Mary that 'those three months were the best I've ever had in my life ... everything came easily and it's still coming easily'.[*]

Like many of the greatest writers, Gibran recognized that the pure spirit of children and the simple language of their discourse were a key to soothing the troubled soul of an adult; as he notes in *Sand and Foam*, 'we often sing lullabies to our children that we ourselves may sleep'.[†] Like Blake, Gibran often chose simple language not out of some imitation of infantilism but because he recognized that simplicity, more often than not, is the most direct path to essential truth.

---

[*]    Quoted in Bushrui and Jenkins 1998, p. 221.
[†]    *Sand and Foam* (Gibran, 1954), p. 17.

# On Giving

Then said a rich man, Speak to us of Giving.
And he answered:
You give but little when you give of your possessions.
It is when you give of yourself that you truly give.
For what are your possessions but things you
    keep and guard for fear you may need them
    tomorrow?
And tomorrow, what shall tomorrow bring to the
    overprudent dog burying bones in the trackless
    sand as he follows the pilgrims to the holy
    city?
And what is fear of need but need itself?
Is not dread of thirst when your well is full, the thirst
    that is unquenchable?

There are those who give little of the much which
    they have – and they give it for recognition
    and their hidden desire makes their gifts
    unwholesome.
And there are those who have little and give it all.
These are the believers in life and the bounty of life,
    and their coffer is never empty.
There are those who give with joy, and that joy is
    their reward.
And there are those who give with pain, and that
    pain is their baptism.
And there are those who give and know not pain
    in giving, nor do they seek joy, nor give with
    mindfulness of virtue;

They give as in yonder valley the myrtle breathes its
fragrance into space.
Through the hands of such as these God speaks,
and from behind their eyes He smiles upon the
earth.

It is well to give when asked, but it is better to give
unasked, through understanding;
And to the open-handed the search for one who shall
receive is joy greater than giving.
And is there aught you would withhold?
All you have shall some day be given;
Therefore give now, that the season of giving may be
yours and not your inheritors'.

You often say, 'I would give, but only to the
deserving.'
The trees in your orchard say not so, nor the flocks in
your pasture. They give that they may live, for to
withhold is to perish.
Surely he who is worthy to receive his days and his
nights, is worthy of all else from you.
And he who has deserved to drink from the ocean
of life deserves to fill his cup from your little
stream.
And what desert greater shall there be, than that
which lies in the courage and the confidence, nay
the charity, of receiving?
And who are you that men should rend their bosom
and unveil their pride, that you may see their
worth naked and their pride unabashed?
See first that you yourself deserve to be a giver, and
an instrument of giving.
For in truth it is life that gives unto life – while you,
who deem yourself a giver, are but a witness.

And you receivers – and you are all receivers – assume
   no weight of gratitude, lest you lay a yoke upon
   yourself and upon him who gives.
Rather rise together with the giver on his gifts as on
   wings,
For to be overmindful of your debt, is to doubt his
   generosity who has the free-hearted earth for
   mother, and God for father.

More of Gibran's views on the subject of giving can be found in his
collection of aphorisms, *Sand and Foam*:

> Generosity is not giving me that which I need more than
> you do, but it is in giving me that which you need more
> than I do.[*]
>
> How mean am I when life gives me gold and I give you silver,
> and yet I deem myself generous.[†]
>
> Generosity is giving more than you can, and pride in taking
> less than you need.[‡]

It is also profitable to compare this sermon with the following passage
from *Jesus, Son of Man*:

> And now let me speak of other things. On a day when
>    He and I were alone walking in a field, we were both
>    hungry, and we came to a wild apple tree.
> There were only two apples hanging on the bough.
> And He held the trunk of the tree with His arm and shook
>    it, and the two apples fell down.
> He picked them both up and he gave one to me. The other
>    He held in His hand.

---

[*]   *Sand and Foam* (Gibran 1954), p. 20.

[†]   *Ibid.*, p. 40.

[‡]   *Ibid.*, p. 61.

In my hunger I ate the apple, and I ate it fast.
Then I looked at Him and I saw that He still held the other
    apple in His hand.
And He gave it to me saying: 'Eat this also.'
And I took the apple, and in my shameless hunger I ate it.
And as we walked on I looked upon His face ...
He had given me the two apples. And I knew He was
    hungry even as I was hungry.
But I now know that in giving them to me He had been
    satisfied.

# On Eating and Drinking

Then an old man, a keeper of an inn, said, Speak to
us of Eating and Drinking.

And he said:

Would that you could live on the fragrance of the
earth, and like an air plant be sustained by the
light.

But since you must kill to eat, and rob the newly born
of its mother's milk to quench your thirst, let it
then be an act of worship.

And let your board stand an altar on which the pure
and the innocent of forest and plain are sacrificed
for that which is purer and still more innocent in
man.

When you kill a beast say to him in your heart,

'By the same power that slays you, I too am slain; and
I too shall be consumed.

For the law that delivered you into my hand shall
deliver me into a mightier hand.

Your blood and my blood is naught but the sap that
feeds the tree of heaven.'

And when you crush an apple with your teeth, say to
it in your heart,

'Your seeds shall live in my body,

And the buds of your tomorrow shall blossom in my
heart,

And your fragrance shall be my breath,

And together we shall rejoice through all the seasons.'

And in the autumn, when you gather the grapes of
    your vineyards for the winepress, say in your
    heart,
'I too am a vineyard, and my fruit shall be gathered
    for the winepress,
And like new wine I shall be kept in eternal vessels.'
And in winter, when you draw the wine, let there be
    in your heart a song for each cup;
And let there be in the song a remembrance for the
    autumn days, and for the vineyard, and for the
    winepress.

Recognizing the inherently ritualistic quality in sustaining existence, this passage both acknowledges the chain of being which shows nature to indeed be 'red in tooth and claw'* and the spiritual aspect which mirrors the Christian Eucharist. The idea of absorbing the spirit of a being through consuming his flesh was found in the belief systems of many tribes, such as those in Africa and Polynesia, and Gibran here interweaves the primal force of life with the holistic, spiritual aspects of nutrition which feed both body and soul.

---

\*    Alfred, Lord Tennyson 2009, p. 236.

# On Work

Then a ploughman said, Speak to us of Work.
And he answered, saying:
You work that you may keep pace with the earth and
    the soul of the earth.
For to be idle is to become a stranger unto the
    seasons, and to step out of life's procession,
    that marches in majesty and proud submission
    towards the infinite.

When you work you are a flute through whose heart
    the whispering of the hours turns to music.
Which of you would be a reed, dumb and silent,
    when all else sings together in unison?

Always you have been told that work is a curse and
    labour a misfortune.
But I say to you that when you work you fulfil a part
    of earth's furthest dream, assigned to you when
    that dream was born,
And in keeping yourself with labour you are in truth
    loving life,
And to love life through labour is to be intimate with
    life's inmost secret.

But if you in your pain call birth an affliction and the
    support of the flesh a curse written upon your
    brow, then I answer that naught but the sweat of
    your brow shall wash away that which is written.

You have been told also that life is darkness, and in your
weariness you echo what was said by the weary.
And I say that life is indeed darkness save when there
is urge,
And all urge is blind save when there is knowledge,
And all knowledge is vain save when there is work,
And all work is empty save when there is love;
And when you work with love you bind yourself to
yourself, and to one another, and to God.

And what is it to work with love?
It is to weave the cloth with threads drawn from your
heart, even as if your beloved were to wear that
cloth.
It is to build a house with affection, even as if your
beloved were to dwell in that house.
It is to sow seeds with tenderness and reap the
harvest with joy, even as if your beloved were to
eat the fruit. It is to charge all things you fashion
with a breath of your own spirit,
And to know that all the blessed dead are standing
about you and watching.

Often have I heard you say, as if speaking in sleep,
'He who works in marble, and finds the shape of
his own soul in the stone, is nobler than he who
ploughs the soil.
And he who seizes the rainbow to lay it on a cloth in
the likeness of man, is more than he who makes
the sandals for our feet.'
But I say, not in sleep but in the overwakefulness of
noontide, that the wind speaks not more sweetly
to the giant oaks than to the least of all the
blades of grass;
And he alone is great who turns the voice of the wind
into a song made sweeter by his own loving.

Work is love made visible.

And if you cannot work with love but only with distaste, it is better that you should leave your work and sit at the gate of the temple and take alms of those who work with joy.

For if you bake bread with indifference, you bake a bitter bread that feeds but half man's hunger.

And if you grudge the crushing of the grapes, your grudge distils a poison in the wine.

And if you sing though as angels, and love not the singing, you muffle man's ears to the voices of the day and the voices of the night.

Gibran celebrates the gift of work, the opportunity to grow, strive and show our spirit – 'work is love made visible' (cf. 'The Master knew no rest except in work. He loved work, which he defined as *Visible Love*').* As with *On Eating and Drinking*, Gibran recognizes the holistic nature of receiving our daily bread, the way in which such daily tasks take on a ritualistic and celebratory aspect which engage us not only with life on earth but with 'the blessed dead' who are present. Again, life works through us – 'when you work you are a flute through whose heart the whispering of the hours turns to music' – and we are further linked in the unity of being.

---

\*    *Treasured Writings* (Gibran 2010), p. 455.

# On Joy and Sorrow

Then a woman said, Speak to us of Joy and
    Sorrow.
And he answered:
Your joy is your sorrow unmasked.
And the selfsame well from which your laughter rises
    was oftentimes filled with your tears.
And how else can it be?
The deeper that sorrow carves into your being, the
    more joy you can contain.
Is not the cup that holds your wine the very cup that
    was burned in the potter's oven?
And is not the lute that soothes your spirit, the very
    wood that was hollowed with knives?
When you are joyous, look deep into your heart and
    you shall find it is only that which has given you
    sorrow that is giving you joy.
When you are sorrowful look again in your heart,
    and you shall see that in truth you are weeping
    for that which has been your delight.

Some of you say, 'Joy is greater than sorrow,' and
    others say, 'Nay, sorrow is the greater.'
But I say unto you, they are inseparable.
Together they come, and when one sits alone with
    you at your board, remember that the other is
    asleep upon your bed.

Verily you are suspended like scales between your
    sorrow and your joy.

Only when you are empty are you at standstill and
    balanced.
When the treasure-keeper lifts you to weigh his
    gold and his silver, needs must your joy or your
    sorrow rise or fall.

Here the influence of Blake is especially felt in a section which recalls
his poem 'The Mental Traveller':

For there the Babe is born in joy
That was begotten in dire woe;
Just as we reap in joy the fruit
Which we in bitter tears did sow.[*]

Once again, Gibran thus underlines the unity of life in showing that joy
and sorrow are two sides of the same coin – an idea also familiar from
Jung's 'shadow' concept and the Chinese 'yin' and 'yang'. As laughter
and tears come from the same source, Gibran suggests that to eliminate
sorrow will also result in becoming joyless. This may go some way to
explaining humankind's fascination with evil, horror and tragedy, in
that it could be a subconscious way of deepening our capacity for joy.

---

[*]    *The Complete Poetry & Prose of William Blake* 1988, pp. 483–484.

# On Houses

Then a mason came forth and said, Speak to us of
    Houses.
And he answered and said:
Build of your imaginings a bower in the wilderness
    ere you build a house within the city walls.
For even as you have home-comings in your twilight, so
    has the wanderer in you, the ever distant and alone.
Your house is your larger body.
It grows in the sun and sleeps in the stillness of the
    night; and it is not dreamless. Does not your
    house dream? and dreaming, leave the city for
    grove or hilltop?

Would that I could gather your houses into my
    hand, and like a sower scatter them in forest and
    meadow.
Would the valleys were your streets, and the green
    paths your alleys, that you might seek one
    another through vineyards, and come with the
    fragrance of the earth in your garments.
But these things are not yet to be.
In their fear your forefathers gathered you too near
    together. And that fear shall endure a little longer.
A little longer shall your city walls separate your
    hearths from your fields.

And tell me, people of Orphalese, what have you
    in these houses? And what is it you guard with
    fastened doors?

Have you peace, the quiet urge that reveals your
    power?
Have you remembrances, the glimmering arches that
    span the summits of the mind?
Have you beauty, that leads the heart from things
    fashioned of wood and stone to the holy
    mountain?
Tell me, have you these in your houses?
Or have you only comfort, and the lust for comfort,
    that stealthy thing that enters the house a guest,
    and then becomes a host, and then a master?

Ay, and it becomes a tamer, and with hook and
    scourge makes puppets of your larger desires.
Though its hands are silken, its heart is of iron.
It lulls you to sleep only to stand by your bed and
    jeer at the dignity of the flesh.
It makes mock of your sound senses, and lays them
    in thistledown like fragile vessels.
Verily the lust for comfort murders the passion of the
    soul, and then walks grinning in the funeral.

But you, children of space, you restless in rest, you
    shall not be trapped nor tamed.
Your house shall be not an anchor but a mast.
It shall not be a glistening film that covers a wound,
    but an eyelid that guards the eye.
You shall not fold your wings that you may pass
    through doors, nor bend your heads that they
    strike not against a ceiling, nor fear to breathe
    lest walls should crack and fall down.
You shall not dwell in tombs made by the dead for
    the living.
And though of magnificence and splendour, your
    house shall not hold your secret nor shelter your
    longing.

For that which is boundless in you abides in the
mansion of the sky, whose door is the morning
mist, and whose windows are the songs and the
silences of the night.

Houses represent the traditions that enslave us, rather than the protection
or enclosure, the world centre or the sheltering aspect of the Great
Mother that a house normally symbolizes. The 'larger body' speaks
of nature, the forest, the world of freedom, while 'children of space'
refers to those who have been freed from the shackles of materialism.
The beautiful, sibilant phrase 'songs and the silences of night' is one
Gibran called to mind when talking of inspiration; as he wrote to Mary
Haskell in January 1909, 'Night is an infinite Sea of thought and dreams'.[*]
Similarly, he wrote to May Ziadah in November 1919 of: 'The silence of
the night when the soul is freed from its shackles and discards its apparel.'[†]

The influence of the Bible may especially be noted in this section:

> Would that I could gather your houses into my hand, and
> like a sower scatter them in forest and meadow.
> Would the valleys were your streets, and the green paths
> your alleys, that you might seek one another through
> vineyards, and come with the fragrance of the earth
> in your garments.
> But these things are not to be.

Here the influence of Christ's lamentation over Jerusalem may be
recalled:

> O Jerusalem, Jerusalem, thou that killest the prophets, and
> stonest them which are sent unto thee, how often would I have
> gathered thy children together, even as a hen gathereth her
> chickens under her wings, and ye would not![‡]

---

[*]    Otto 1963, p. 19.
[†]    Bushrui and al-Kuzbari 1995, p. 23.
[‡]    Matt. 23:37.

# On Clothes

And the weaver said, Speak to us of Clothes.
And he answered:
Your clothes conceal much of your beauty, yet they
    hide not the unbeautiful.
And though you seek in garments the freedom of
    privacy you may find in them a harness and a
    chain.
Would that you could meet the sun and the wind
    with more of your skin and less of your raiment,
For the breath of life is in the sunlight and the hand
    of life is in the wind.

Some of you say, 'It is the north wind who has woven
    the clothes we wear.'
And I say, Ay, it was the north wind,
But shame was his loom, and the softening of the
    sinews was his thread.
And when his work was done he laughed in the
    forest.
Forget not that modesty is for a shield against the eye
    of the unclean.
And when the unclean shall be no more, what were
    modesty but a fetter and a fouling of the mind?
And forget not that the earth delights to feel your
    bare feet and the winds long to play with your
    hair.

In this sermon, which makes much use of symbolism, 'clothes' refer to (attachment to) obsolete traditions, 'sun and wind' to liberty and freedom, while the 'north wind' mirrors the power of enslaving traditions.

Blakean imagery is also much in evidence in this section:

> Some of you say, 'It is the north wind who has woven the
>     clothes we wear.'
> And I say, Ay, it was the north wind,
> But shame was his loom, and the softening of the sinews
>     was his thread,
> And when his work was done he laughed in the forest.

Here we are reminded of the metaphysical poetry of Blake – particularly his use of personification and the image of the forest as the abode of the spiritually awakened:

> ... what art
> Could twist the sinews of thy heart? ...
> When the stars threw down their spears,
> And water'd heaven with their tears,
> Did he smile his work to see?
> Did he who made the lamb make thee?
>
> Tyger! Tyger! burning bright
> In the forests of the night*

* *The Complete Poetry & Prose of William Blake* 1988, p. 25.

# On Buying and Selling

And a merchant said, Speak to us of Buying and
　　　Selling.
And he answered and said:
To you the earth yields her fruit, and you shall
　　　not want if you but know how to fill your
　　　hands.
It is in exchanging the gifts of the earth that you shall
　　　find abundance and be satisfied.
Yet unless the exchange be in love and kindly justice,
　　　it will but lead some to greed and others to
　　　hunger.

When in the market place you toilers of the sea and
　　　fields and vineyards meet the weavers and the
　　　potters and the gatherers of spices, –
Invoke then the master spirits of the earth, to
　　　come into your midst and sanctify the scales
　　　and the reckoning that weighs value against
　　　value.

And suffer not the barren-handed to take part in your
　　　transactions, who would sell their words for
　　　your labour.
To such men you should say,
'Come with us to the field, or go with our brothers to
　　　the sea and cast your net;
For the land and the sea shall be bountiful to you
　　　even as to us.'

And if there come the singers and the dancers and
the flute players, – buy of their gifts also.
For they too are the gatherers of fruit and
frankincense, and that which they bring, though
fashioned of dreams, is raiment and food for
your soul.

And before you leave the market place, see that no
one has gone his way with empty hands.
For the master spirit of the earth shall not sleep
peacefully upon the wind till the needs of the
least of you are satisfied.

As with *On Eating and Drinking*, Gibran emphasizes that it is as
much the spirit as the body which must be fulfilled. In this way, those
who enrich the soul, such as singers, dancers and musicians, are equal
to purveyors of food. He reserves his censure for those who nourish
neither, those who would 'sell their words', such as landlords, capitalists
and bankers. There should be labour, transfer of nature, with truly
heartening products in exchange. Fairness is paramount, as Gibran
also illustrated in the following passage from *The Voice of the Master*:

Are you a merchant, drawing advantage from the needs of the
people, engrossing goods so as to resell them at an exorbitant
price? If so, you are a reprobate; and it matters naught whether
your home is a palace or a prison.

Or are you an honest man, who enables farmer and weaver
to exchange their products, who mediates between buyer and
seller, and through his just ways profits both himself and others?
If so, you are a righteous man; and it matters not whether you
are praised or blamed. *

---

\*     *The Voice of the Master* (Gibran 1958), p. 34.

# On Crime and Punishment

Then one of the judges of the city stood forth and
    said, Speak to us of Crime and Punishment.
And he answered, saying:
It is when your spirit goes wandering upon the
    wind,
That you, alone and unguarded, commit a wrong
    unto others and therefore yourself.
And for that wrong committed must you knock and
    wait a while unheeded at the gate of the blessed.

Like the ocean is your god-self;
It remains for ever undefiled.
And like the ether it lifts but the winged.
Even like the sun is your god-self;
It knows not the ways of the mole nor seeks it the
    holes of the serpent.
But your god-self dwells not alone in your being.
Much in you is still man, and much in you is not yet
    man,
But a shapeless pigmy that walks asleep in the mist
    searching for its own awakening.
And of the man in you would I now speak.
For it is he and not your god-self nor the pigmy in
    the mist, that knows crime and the punishment
    of crime.
Oftentimes have I heard you speak of one who
    commits a wrong as though he were not one of
    you, but a stranger unto you and an intruder
    upon your world.

But I say that even as the holy and righteous cannot rise
beyond the highest which is in each one of you,
So the wicked and the weak cannot fall lower than
the lowest which is in you also.
And as a single leaf turns not yellow but with the
silent knowledge of the whole tree,
So the wrong-doer cannot do wrong without the
hidden will of you all.
Like a procession you walk together towards your
god-self.
You are the way and the wayfarers.
And when one of you falls down he falls for those
behind him, a caution against the stumbling stone.
Ay, and he falls for those ahead of him, who though
faster and surer of foot, yet removed not the
stumbling stone.

And this also, though the word lie heavy upon your
hearts:
The murdered is not unaccountable for his own murder,
And the robbed is not blameless in being robbed.
The righteous is not innocent of the deeds of the
wicked,
And the white-handed is not clean in the doings of
the felon.
Yea, the guilty is oftentimes the victim of the injured,
And still more often the condemned is the burden
bearer for the guiltless and unblamed.
You cannot separate the just from the unjust and the
good from the wicked;
For they stand together before the face of the sun
even as the black thread and the white are woven
together.
And when the black thread breaks, the weaver shall
look into the whole cloth, and he shall examine
the loom also.

If any of you would bring to judgement the unfaithful
    wife,
Let him also weigh the heart of her husband in scales,
    and measure his soul with measurements.
And let him who would lash the offender look unto the
    spirit of the offended.
And if any of you would punish in the name of
    righteousness and lay the axe unto the evil tree, let
    him see to its roots;
And verily he will find the roots of the good and the bad,
    the fruitful and the fruitless, all entwined together in
    the silent heart of the earth.
And you judges who would be just,
What judgement pronounce you upon him who though
    honest in the flesh is yet a thief in spirit?
What penalty lay you upon him who slays in the flesh yet
    is himself slain in the spirit?
And prosecute you him who in action is a deceiver and
    oppressor,
Yet who is also aggrieved and outraged?

And how shall you punish those whose remorse is already
    greater than their misdeeds?
Is not remorse the justice which is administered by that
    very law which you would fain serve?
Yet you cannot lay remorse upon the innocent nor lift it
    from the heart of the guilty.
Unbidden shall it call in the night, that men may wake
    and gaze upon themselves.
And you who would understand justice, how shall you
    unless you look upon all deeds in the fullness of light?
Only then shall you know that the erect and the fallen
    are but one man standing in the twilight between the
    night of his pigmy-self and the day of his god-self,
And that the corner stone of the temple is not higher
    than the lowest stone in its foundation.

This section of *The Prophet*, with its central theme of 'what collective humanity does is done by each of us', was one of the earliest to be discussed with Mary Haskell.[*] Gibran first presented it to her in April 1920. Upon its completion, they went over it together with meticulous care, changing only the occasional word.[†]

This is in many ways one of the most controversial sections of *The Prophet*. The concept that all men are to blame for the wrongdoing of an individual may seem a harsh and uncompromising stance, but such an idea concerning the inherent unity of humankind speaks of great compassion. Gibran wrote to May Ziadah in November 1919 that 'any crime is in itself a punishment for the criminal'[‡] and the mention of the Almighty to whom all souls yearn comes almost immediately with 'like the ocean is your god-self' in the second stanza. Human life is full of suffering but we are thus reminded that the Almighty is always with us, even when we perceive ourselves to be 'alone and unguarded'. In this second stanza, all life is encapsulated – god-self, man-self and animal-self.

Gibran's use of 'pigmy' is a symbolic reference to youth, immaturity and innocence as in Wordsworth's 'Ode: Intimations of Immortality from Recollections of Early Childhood':

> Behold the Child among his new-born blisses,
> A six years' Darling of pigmy size![§]

This sermon especially highlights how central the Súfí concept of *wahdat al-wudjud* (unity of being) was to Gibran's thought. 'Like a procession you walk together towards your god-self' – this above all speaks of the path that men must traverse in a quest towards the central god-head.[¶] Similarly, the spirit of Christ is invoked:

---

[*]   Hilu 1972, p. 331.
[†]   *Ibid.*, p. 339.
[‡]   Bushrui and al-Kuzbari 1995, p. 20.
[§]   In Quiller-Couch, 1919.
[¶]   See the section entitled '"Yearning" and the Súfí Idea of Journeying', p. xlvii.

'If any of you would bring to judgement the
    unfaithful wife,
Let him also weigh the heart of her husband in scales, and
    measure his soul with measurements.'

Who can read this passage without recalling the biblical verse 'He that is without sin among you, let him cast the first stone' (John 8:7)?

This sermon speaks squarely and democratically about the terrible injustice of 'justice' – not just as it relates to fairness in discovering truth and laying out a penalty, but to the larger issue of real causality and responsibility.

# On Laws

Then a lawyer said, But what of our Laws, master?
And he answered:
You delight in laying down laws,
Yet you delight more in breaking them.
Like children playing by the ocean who build sand-
    towers with constancy and then destroy them with
    laughter.
But while you build your sand-towers the ocean brings
    more sand to the shore,
And when you destroy them the ocean laughs with you.
Verily the ocean laughs always with the innocent.

But what of those to whom life is not an ocean, and
    man-made laws are not sand-towers,
But to whom life is a rock, and the law a chisel with
    which they would carve it in their own likeness?
What of the cripple who hates dancers?
What of the ox who loves his yoke and deems the elk
    and the deer of the forest stray and vagrant things?
What of the old serpent who cannot shed his skin, and
    calls all others naked and shameless?
And of him who comes early to the wedding-feast, and
    when over-fed and tired goes his way saying that
    all feasts are violation and all feasters lawbreakers?

What shall I say of these save that they too stand in the
    sunlight, but with their backs to the sun?
They see only their shadows, and their shadows are
    their laws.

And what is the sun to them but a caster of shadows?

And what is it to acknowledge the laws but to stoop
down and trace their shadows upon the earth?

But you who walk facing the sun, what images drawn
on the earth can hold you?

You who travel with the wind, what weather-vane shall
direct your course?

What man's law shall bind you if you break your yoke
but upon no man's prison door?

What laws shall you fear if you dance but stumble
against no man's iron chains?

And who is he that shall bring you to judgement if you
tear off your garment yet leave it in no man's path?


People of Orphalese, you can muffle the drum, and you
can loosen the strings of the lyre, but who shall
command the skylark not to sing?

Closely related to *On Crime and Punishment,* it would seem to follow
on reading this text that the conditions for criminal action, prompting it,
should be removed. Give a man dignity, protection, freedom and love and
he will not harm others. In his earlier work, *al-Arwah al-Mutamarridah*
(*Spirits Rebellious*), Gibran wrote:

> Everything on earth lives according to the law of nature, and
> from that law emerges the glory and joy of liberty; but man
> is denied this fortune, because he set for the God-given soul
> a limited and earthly law of his own. He made for himself
> strict rules. Man built a narrow and painful prison in which he
> secluded his affections and desire. He dug out a deep grave in
> which he buried his heart and its purpose.[*]

---

[*]    *Spirits Rebellious* (Gibran 1947), p. 28.

# On Freedom

And an orator said, Speak to us of Freedom,
And he answered:
At the city gate and by your fireside I have seen
  you prostrate yourself and worship your own
  freedom,
Even as slaves humble themselves before a tyrant and
  praise him though he slays them.
Ay, in the grove of the temple and in the shadow of
  the citadel I have seen the freest among you wear
  their freedom as a yoke and a handcuff.
And my heart bled within me; for you can only be
  free when even the desire of seeking freedom
  becomes a harness to you, and when you cease
  to speak of freedom as a goal and a fulfilment.

You shall be free indeed when your days are not
  without a care nor your nights without a want
  and a grief,
But rather when these things girdle your life and yet
  you rise above them naked and unbound.

And how shall you rise beyond your days and nights
  unless you break the chains which you at the
  dawn of your understanding have fastened
  around your noon hour?
In truth that which you call freedom is the strongest
  of these chains, though its links glitter in the sun
  and dazzle your eyes.

And what is it but fragments of your own self you
would discard that you may become free?
If it is an unjust law you would abolish, that law
was written with your own hand upon you own
forehead.
You cannot erase it by burning your law books nor
by washing the foreheads of your judges, though
you pour the sea upon them.
And if it is a despot you would dethrone, see
first that his throne erected within you is
destroyed.
For how can a tyrant rule the free and the proud, but
for a tyranny in their own freedom and a shame
in their own pride?
And if it is a care you would cast off, that care has
been chosen by you rather than imposed upon
you.
And if it is a fear you would dispel, the seat of that
fear is in your heart and not in the hand of the
feared.

Verily all things move within your being in constant
half embrace, the desired and the dreaded, the
repugnant and the cherished, the pursued and
that which you would escape.
These things move within you as lights and shadows
in pairs that cling.
And when the shadow fades and is no more,
the light that lingers becomes a shadow to
another light.
And thus your freedom when it loses its fetters
becomes itself the fetter of a greater freedom.

Gibran's views on freedom can also be gleaned from *The Voice of the Master*, from which the following extracts come:

> Freedom bids us to her table where we may partake of her savoury food and rich wine; but when we sit down at her board, we eat ravenously and glut ourselves.[*]

> God has given you a spirit with wings on which to soar into the spacious firmament of Love and Freedom. Is it not pitiful then that you cut your wings with your own hands and suffer your soul to crawl like an insect upon the earth?[†]

---

[*]    *The Voice of the Master* (Gibran 1958), p. 46.

[†]    *Ibid.*, p. 68.

# On Reason and Passion

And the priestess spoke again and said, Speak to us of
  Reason and Passion.
And he answered, saying:
Your soul is oftentimes a battlefield, upon which your
  reason and your judgement wage war against your
  passion and your appetite.
Would that I could be the peacemaker in your soul, that
  I might turn the discord and the rivalry of your
  elements into oneness and melody.
But how shall I, unless you yourselves be also the
  peacemakers, nay, the lovers of all your elements?

Your reason and your passion are the rudder and the
  sails of your seafaring soul.
If either your sails or your rudder be broken, you can
  but toss and drift, or else be held at a standstill in
  mid-seas.
For reason, ruling alone, is a force confining; and
  passion, unattended, is a flame that burns to its
  own destruction.
Therefore let your soul exalt your reason to the height
  of passion, that it may sing;
And let it direct your passion with reason, that your
  passion may live through its own daily resurrection,
  and like the phoenix rise above its own ashes.

I would have you consider your judgement and your
  appetite even as you would two loved guests in your
  house.

Surely you would not honour one guest above the other;
for he who is more mindful of one loses the love
and the faith of both.

Among the hills, when you sit in the cool shade of the
white poplars, sharing the peace and serenity of
distant fields and meadows – then let your heart
say in silence, 'God rests in reason.'
And when the storm comes, and the mighty wind
shakes the forest, and thunder and lightning
proclaim the majesty of the sky, – then let your
heart say in awe, 'God moves in passion.'
And since you are a breath in God's sphere, and a leaf
in God's forest, you too should rest in reason and
move in passion.

Among the hills, when you sit in the cool shade of the
white poplars, sharing the peace and serenity of
distant fields and meadows – then let your heart say
in silence, 'God rests in reason.'
And when the storm comes, and the mighty wind shakes
the forest, and the thunder and lightning proclaim the
majesty of the sky, – then let your heart say in awe,
'God moves in passion.'
And since you are a breath in God's sphere, and a leaf in
God's forest, you too should rest in reason and move
in passion.

This section above all in *The Prophet* displays the influence of the
Romantic vision on Gibran. The strong landscape evoked and the
cinematic quality, as well the intertwining of nature and the spirit, call
to mind not only the work of the Romantic poets but also the images
of such Romantic artists as Caspar David Friedrich.

# On Pain

And a woman spoke, saying, Tell us of Pain.
And he said:
Your pain is the breaking of the shell that encloses
    your understanding.
Even as the stone of the fruit must break, that its
    heart may stand in the sun, so must you know
    pain.
And could you keep your heart in wonder at the daily
    miracles of your life, your pain would not seem
    less wondrous than your joy;
And you would accept the seasons of your heart,
    even as you have always accepted the seasons
    that pass over your fields.
And you would watch with serenity through the
    winters of your grief.

Much of your pain is self-chosen.
It is the bitter potion by which the physician within
    you heals your sick self.
Therefore trust the physician, and drink his remedy
    in silence and tranquillity:
For his hand, though heavy and hard, is guided by
    the tender hand of the Unseen,
And the cup he brings, though it burn your lips, has
    been fashioned of the clay which the Potter has
    moistened with His own sacred tears.

Gibran certainly believed in the value of pain; prefiguring C.S. Lewis in his views and echoing the sentiments of *On Joy and Sorrow*, Gibran wrote to Mary Haskell in June 1923:

> Pain can be very creative ... I suffered a great deal through you and you suffered a great deal through me. But that pain brought us to the big thing in life. We lived more because of it than because of anything else.[*]

'How shall my heart be unsealed unless it be broken?' wrote Gibran in *Sand and Foam*[†] – reminiscent of Oscar Wilde's cry, 'how else but through a broken heart may Lord Christ enter in?'[‡]

*    Hilu 1972, p. 411.
†    *Sand and Foam* (Gibran 1954), p. 23.
‡    *The Collected Works of Oscar Wilde* 2007, vol. 4, p. 908.

# On Self-Knowledge

And a man said, Speak to us of Self-
    Knowledge.
And he answered, saying:
Your hearts know in silence the secrets of the
    days and the nights.
But your ears thirst for the sound of your
    heart's knowledge.
You would know in words that which you
    have always known in thought.
You would touch with your fingers the naked
    body of your dreams.

And it is well you should.
The hidden well-spring of your soul must
    needs rise and run murmuring to the sea;
And the treasure of your infinite depths
    would be revealed to your eyes.
But let there be no scales to weigh your
    unknown treasure;
And seek not the depths of your knowledge
    with staff or sounding line.
For self is a sea boundless and measureless.

Say not, 'I have found the truth,' but rather, 'I
    have found a truth.'
Say not, 'I have found the path of the soul.'
    Say rather, 'I have met the soul walking
    upon my path.'
For the soul walks upon all paths.

The soul walks not upon a line, neither does
 it grow like a reed.
The soul unfolds itself, like a lotus of
 countless petals.

Like the subject matter itself, the argument is there before our eyes
with only the symbolism of 'well-spring' – eventful life of mysteries
unceasing and unfathomable – requiring translation. What at first may
appear complicated, or beyond our ken, is there to be seen, both in the
core of us and all around us.

# On Teaching

Then said a teacher, Speak to us of Teaching.

And he said:

No man can reveal to you aught but that which already lies half asleep in the dawning of your knowledge.

The teacher who walks in the shadow of the temple, among his followers, gives not of his wisdom but rather of his faith and his lovingness.

If he is indeed wise he does not bid you enter the house of his wisdom, but rather leads you to the threshold of your own mind.

The astronomer may speak to you of his understanding of space, but he cannot give you his understanding.

The musician may sing to you of the rhythm which is in all space, but he cannot give you the ear which arrests the rhythm nor the voice that echoes it.

And he who is versed in the science of numbers can tell of the regions of weight and measure, but he cannot conduct you thither.

For the vision of one man lends not its wings to another man.

And even as each one of you stands alone in God's knowledge, so must each one of you be alone in his knowledge of God and in his understanding of the earth.

As with *On Self-Knowledge*, Gibran points out that truth and understanding are already within us. The influence of Emerson's 'self-reliance' can be detected here. Although we need teachers to show us the way and to illuminate teachings, we must not accept wholesale the vision of a guru or a dogma but rather explore these for ourselves.

# On Friendship

And a youth said, Speak to us of Friendship.
And he answered, saying:
Your friend is your needs answered.
He is your field which you sow with love and reap
    with thanksgiving.
And he is your board and your fireside.
For you come to him with your hunger, and you seek
    him for peace.

When your friend speaks his mind you fear not the 'nay'
    in your own mind, nor do you withhold the 'ay'.
And when he is silent your heart ceases not to listen
    to his heart.
For without words, in friendship, all thoughts, all
    desires, all expectations are born and shared,
    with joy that is unacclaimed.
When you part from your friend, you grieve him not;
For that which you love most in him may be clearer
    in his absence, as the mountain to the climber is
    clearer from the plain.
And let there be no purpose in friendship save the
    deepening of the spirit.
For love that seeks aught but the disclosure of its own
    mystery is not love but a net cast forth; and only
    the unprofitable is caught.

And let your best be for your friend.
If he must know the ebb of your tide, let him know
    its flood also.

For what is your friend that you should seek him
    with hours to kill?
Seek him always with hours to live.
For it is his to fill your need, but not your emptiness.
And in the sweetness of friendship let there be
    laughter, and sharing of pleasures.
For in the dew of little things the heart finds its
    morning and is refreshed.

It is clear from the deep and meaningful friendships that Gibran formed throughout his life that friendship was passionately important to him. He wrote to Carlous Verhulst on 10 May 1927:

> I am indeed happy that it is in your gracious desire to call me *your friend*. I would rather be a friend, your friend, than anything else in the world. To me friendship is the only sound foundation of all human relationships.[*]

It is notable that Gibran's most significant friendships were all with women: Mary Haskell, the collaborator and benefactress to whom he proposed marriage; Barbara Young, his secretary and companion during the last years of his life; May Ziadah, with whom he established an extraordinary literary and love relationship expressed purely in letters without ever meeting her.

---

[*]     Unpublished letter, courtesy of Mr Verhulst.

# On Talking

And then a scholar said, Speak of Talking.
And he answered, saying:
You talk when you cease to be at peace with your
    thoughts;
And when you can no longer dwell in the solitude of
    your heart you live in your lips, and sound is a
    diversion and a pastime.
And in much of your talking, thinking is half
    murdered.
For thought is a bird of space, that in a cage of words
    may indeed unfold its wings but cannot fly.

There are those among you who seek the talkative
    through fear of being alone.
The silence of aloneness reveals to their eyes their
    naked selves and they would escape.
And there are those who talk, and without
    knowledge or forethought reveal a truth which
    they themselves do not understand.
And there are those who have the truth within them
    but they tell it not in words.
In the bosom of such as these the spirit dwells in
    rhythmic silence.

When you meet your friend on the roadside or in the
    market place, let the spirit in you move your lips
    and direct your tongue.
Let the voice within your voice speak to the ear of his
    ear,

For his soul will keep the truth of your heart as the
    taste of the wine is remembered
When the colour is forgotten and the vessel is no
    more.

'The ear of his ear' refers to insight. Gibran wrote to May Ziadah in February 1919:

> I have always known that behind your ears lie other hidden ears which can hear those very fine sounds that are so much like silence – those sounds, not created by lips and tongues but which emanate from behind tongues and lips, sounds of sweet loneliness, of pleasure and pain, and of longing for that unknown and distant word.[*]

---

\*    Bushrui and al-Kuzbari 1995, p. 8.

# On Time

And an astronomer said, Master, what of Time?
And he answered:
You would measure time the measureless and the
    immeasurable.
You would adjust your conduct and even direct the
    course of your spirit according to hours and
    seasons.
Of time you would make a stream upon whose bank
    you would sit and watch its flowing.

Yet the timeless in you is aware of life's timelessness,
And knows that yesterday is but today's memory and
    tomorrow is today's dream.
And that that which sings and contemplates in you
    is still dwelling within the bounds of that first
    moment which scattered the stars into space.
Who among you does not feel that his power to love is
    boundless?
And yet who does not feel that very love, though
    boundless, encompassed within the centre of his
    being, and moving not from love thought to love
    thought, nor from love deed to other love deeds?
And is not time even as love is, undivided and spaceless?

But if in your thought you must measure time into
    seasons, let each season encircle all the other seasons,
And let today embrace the past with remembrance and
    the future with longing.

This section can profitably be compared to the following from Gibran's *Thoughts and Meditations*:

> My soul spoke to me and said, 'Do not measure Time
>     by saying, "There was yesterday, and there shall be
>     tomorrow."
> And ere my soul spoke to me, I imagined the Past as an
>     epoch that never returned, and the Future as one that
>     could never be reached.
> Now I realize that the present moment contains all time
>     and within it is all that can be hoped for, done and
>     realized.[*]

---

[*]    *Thoughts and Meditations* (Gibran 1960), p. 30.

# On Good and Evil

And one of the elders of the city said, Speak to us of
    Good and Evil.
And he answered:
Of the good in you can I speak, but not of the evil.
For what is evil but good tortured by its own hunger
    and thirst?
Verily when good is hungry it seeks food even in dark
    caves, and when it thirsts it drinks even of dead
    waters.

You are good when you are one with yourself.
Yet when you are not one with yourself you are not
    evil.
For a divided house is not a den of thieves; it is only
    a divided house.
And a ship without a rudder may wander aimlessly
    among perilous isles yet sink not to the bottom.

You are good when you strive to give of yourself.
Yet you are not evil when you seek gain for
    yourself.
For when you strive for gain you are but a root that
    clings to the earth and sucks at her breast.
Surely the fruit cannot say to the root, 'Be like
    me, ripe and full and ever giving of your
    abundance.'
For to the fruit giving is a need, as receiving is a need
    to the root.

You are good when you are fully awake in your
    speech,
Yet you are not evil when you sleep while your tongue
    staggers without purpose.
And even stumbling speech may strengthen a weak
    tongue.

You are good when you walk to your goal firmly and
    with bold steps.
Yet you are not evil when you go thither limping.
Even those who limp go not backward.
But you who are strong and swift, see that you do not
    limp before the lame, deeming it kindness.

You are good in countless ways, and you are not evil
    when you are not good,
You are only loitering and sluggard.
Pity that the stags cannot teach swiftness to the
    turtles.

In your longing for your giant self lies your goodness
    and that longing is in all of you.
But in some of you that longing is a torrent rushing
    with might to the sea, carrying the secrets of the
    hillsides and the songs of the forest.
And in others it is a flat stream that loses itself in
    angles and bends and lingers before it reaches
    the shore.
But let not him who longs much say to him who
    longs little, 'Wherefore are you slow and
    halting?'
For the truly good ask not the naked, 'Where is your
    garment?' nor the homeless, 'What has befallen
    your house?'

The influence of Blake can again be detected in this passage, where 'for what is evil but good tortured by its own hunger and thirst?' echoes Blake's 'evil is good that has been parched by thirst and starved by hunger'.* The evocation of the 'giant self' is the Almighty towards whom all souls yearn.

---

*     *Complete Writings of William Blake* 1966, p. 540.

# On Prayer

Then a priestess said, Speak to us of Prayer.
And he answered, saying:
You pray in your distress and in your need, would
     that you might pray also in the fullness of
     your joy and in your days of abundance.

For what is prayer but the expansion of yourself
     into the living ether?
And if it is for your comfort to pour your
     darkness into space, it is also for your delight
     to pour forth the dawning of your heart.
And if you cannot but weep when your soul
     summons you to prayer, she should spur you
     again and yet again, though weeping, until
     you shall come laughing.
When you pray you rise to meet in the air those
     who are praying at that very hour, and whom
     save in prayer you may not meet.
Therefore let your visit to that temple invisible
     be for naught but ecstasy and sweet
     communion.
For if you should enter the temple for no other
     purpose than asking you shall not receive:
And if you should enter into it to humble yourself
     you shall not be lifted:
Or even if you should enter into it to beg for the
     good of others you shall not be heard.
It is enough that you enter the temple invisible.

I cannot teach you how to pray in words.

God listens not to your words save when He
Himself utters them through your lips.

And I cannot teach you the prayer of the seas and
the forests and the mountains.

But you who are born of the mountains and the
forests and the seas can find their prayer in
your heart,

And if you but listen in the stillness of the night
you shall hear them saying in silence,

'Oh God, who art our winged self, it is thy will in
us that willeth.

It is thy desire in us that desireth.

It is thy urge in us that would turn our nights,
which are thine, into days which are thine
also.

We cannot ask thee for aught, for thou knowest
our needs before they are born in us:

Thou art our need; and in giving us more of
thyself thou givest us all.'

'God listens not to your words save when He Himself utters them through your lips' is reminiscent of one of the sayings of the Prophet Muhammad recorded in a Hadith:

A servant draws near to me in prayer when I become the eyes with which he sees and the ears with which he hears.[*]

This same sermon contains a passage which is close to Súfí doctrine:

And if you but listen in the stillness of the night you shall
hear them saying in silence,

*     Bushrui 1989, p. 55.

'Our God, who are our winged self, it is thy will in us that willeth.

It is thy desire in us that desireth.

It is thy urge in us that would turn our nights, which are thine, into days which are thine also.

We cannot ask thee for aught, for thou knowest our needs before they are born in us;

Thou art our need; and in giving us more of thyself thou givest us all.'

# On Pleasure

Then a hermit, who visited the city once a year,
　　came forth and said, Speak to us of Pleasure.
And he answered, saying:
Pleasure is a freedom-song,
But it is not freedom.
It is the blossoming of your desires,
But it is not their fruit.
It is a depth calling unto a height,
But it is not the deep nor the high.
It is the caged taking wing,
But it is not space encompassed.
Ay, in very truth, pleasure is a freedom-song.
And I fain would have you sing it with fullness
　　of heart; yet I would not have you lose your
　　hearts in the singing.

Some of your youth seek pleasure as if it were all,
　　and they are judged and rebuked.
I would not judge nor rebuke them. I would have
　　them seek.
For they shall find pleasure, but not her alone;
Seven are her sisters, and the least of them is
　　more beautiful than pleasure.
Have you not heard of the man who was digging
　　in the earth for roots and found a treasure?

And some of your elders remember pleasures
　　with regret like wrongs committed in
　　drunkenness.

But regret is the beclouding of the mind and not
      its chastisement.
They should remember their pleasures with
      gratitude, as they would the harvest of a
      summer.
Yet if it comforts them to regret, let them be
      comforted.

And there are among you those who are neither
      young to seek nor old to remember;
And in their fear of seeking and remembering
      they shun all pleasures, lest they neglect the
      spirit or offend against it.
But even in their foregoing is their pleasure.
And thus they too find a treasure though they dig
      for roots with quivering hands.
But tell me, who is he that can offend the spirit?
Shall the nightingale offend the stillness of the
      night, or the firefly the stars?
And shall your flame or your smoke burden the
      wind?
Think you the spirit is a still pool which you can
      trouble with a staff?

Oftentimes in denying yourself pleasure you do
      but store the desire in the recesses of your
      being.

Who knows but that which seems omitted today,
      waits for tomorrow?
Even your body knows its heritage and its
      rightful need and will not be deceived.
And your body is the harp of your soul,
And it is yours to bring forth sweet music from it
      or confused sounds.

And now you ask in your heart, 'How shall we
    distinguish that which is good in pleasure
    from that which is not good?'
Go to your fields and your gardens, and you shall
    learn that it is the pleasure of the bee to
    gather honey of the flower,
But it is also the pleasure of the flower to yield its
    honey to the bee.
For to the bee a flower is a fountain of life,
And to the flower a bee is a messenger of love,
And to both, bee and flower, the giving and
    the receiving of pleasure is a need and an
    ecstasy.

People of Orphalese, be in your pleasures like the
    flowers and the bees.

The spirit of Blake can once again be sensed in this passage on pleasure;
the hedonistic-sounding aphorism in *The Marriage of Heaven and Hell*
'he who desires but acts not, breeds pestilence'* may have provided the
inspiration for the line in this sermon:

Oftentimes in denying yourself pleasure you do but store
    the desire in the recesses of your being.

---

*    *The Complete Poetry & Prose of William Blake* 1988, p. 35.

# On Beauty

And a poet said, Speak to us of Beauty.
And he answered:
Where shall you seek beauty, and how shall you find
    her unless she herself be your way and your guide?
And how shall you speak of her except she be the
    weaver of your speech?

The aggrieved and the injured say, 'Beauty is kind
    and gentle.
Like a young mother half-shy of her own glory she
    walks among us.'
And the passionate say, 'Nay, beauty is a thing of
    might and dread.
Like the tempest she shakes the earth beneath us and
    the sky above us.'

The tired and the weary say, 'Beauty is of soft
    whisperings. She speaks in our spirit.
Her voice yields to our silences like a faint light that
    quivers in fear of the shadow.'
But the restless say, 'We have heard her shouting
    among the mountains,
And with her cries came the sound of hoofs, and the
    beating of wings and the roar of lions.'

At night the watchmen of the city say, 'Beauty shall
    rise with the dawn from the east.'
And at noontide the toilers and the wayfarers say,
    'We have seen her leaning over the earth from
    the windows of the sunset.'

In winter the snow-bound say, 'She shall come with
      the spring leaping upon the hills.'
And in the summer heat the reapers say, 'We have
      seen her dancing with the autumn leaves, and we
      saw a drift of snow in her hair.'
All these things have you said of beauty,
Yet in truth you spoke not of her but of needs
      unsatisfied,
And beauty is not a need but an ecstasy.
It is not a mouth thirsting nor an empty hand
      stretched forth,
But rather a heart enflamed and a soul enchanted.
It is not the image you would see nor the song you
      would hear,
But rather an image you see though you close your eyes
      and a song you hear though you shut your ears.
It is not the sap within the furrowed bark, nor a wing
      attached to a claw,
But rather a garden for ever in bloom and a flock of
      angels for ever in flight.

People of Orphalese, beauty is life when life unveils
      her holy face.
But you are life and you are the veil.
Beauty is eternity gazing at itself in a mirror.
But you are eternity and you are the mirror.

The language of the King James Bible is especially prominent in this
sermon:

    At night the watchmen of the city say, 'Beauty shall rise
        with the dawn from the east.'

And at noontide the toilers and the wayfarers say, 'We have
   seen her leaning over the earth from the windows of
   the sunset.'
In winter say the snow-bound, 'She shall come with the
   spring leaping upon the hills.'
And in the summer heat the reapers say, 'We have seen her
   dancing with the autumn leaves, and we saw a drift of
   snow in her hair.'

This calls to mind the incantational Song of Solomon:

My beloved spake, and said unto me, Rise up, my love, my
   fair one, and come away.
For, lo, the winter is past, the rain is over and gone;
The flowers appear on the earth; the time of the singing of
   birds is come, and the voice of the turtle is heard in
   our land ...
The watchmen that go about the city found me: to whom I
   said, Saw ye him whom my soul loveth?[*]

The symbolism of the 'veil' in this section refers to mind, ignorance and
unknowing. Gibran wrote to May Ziadah in May 1922 that 'each one of
us is veiled with a thousand veils'.[†] The veil is another universal symbol
as in Islam it represents hidden knowledge and revelation; in Christianity
it symbolizes modesty, chastity, worldly renunciation; in Buddhism and
Hinduism, *maya* is the veil of illusion that obscures reality.

Gibran's thoughts on beauty and humankind's attitude to it can
also be found in *The Voice of the Master*:

Beauty reveals herself to us as she sits on the throne of glory;
but we approach her in the name of Lust, snatch off her crown
of purity, and pollute her garment with our evil-doing.[‡]

---

[*]   Song of Solomon 2:10–12 and 3:3.
[†]   Bushrui and al-Kuzbari 1995, p. 56.
[‡]   *The Voice of the Master* (Gibran 1958), p. 46.

# On Religion

And an old priest said, Speak to us of Religion.
And he said:
Have I spoken this day of aught else?
Is not religion all deeds and all reflection,
And that which is neither deed nor reflection, but
    a wonder and a surprise ever springing in the
    soul, even while the hands hew the stone or
    tend the loom?
Who can separate his faith from his actions, or his
    belief from his occupations?
Who can spread his hours before him, saying, 'This
    for God and this for myself; This for my soul,
    and this other for my body?'
All your hours are wings that beat through space
    from self to self.
He who wears his morality but as his best garment
    were better naked.
The wind and the sun will tear no holes in his skin.
And he who defines his conduct by ethics imprisons
    his song-bird in a cage.
The freest song comes not through bars and wires.
And he to whom worshipping is a window, to open
    but also to shut, has not yet visited the house of
    his soul whose windows are from dawn to dawn.

Your daily life is your temple and your religion.
Whenever you enter into it take with you your all.
Take the plough and the forge and the mallet and the
    lute,

The things you have fashioned in necessity or for
    delight.
For in reverie you cannot rise above your
    achievements nor fall lower than your failures.
And take with you all men:
For in adoration you cannot fly higher than their
    hopes nor humble yourself lower than their
    despair.


And if you would know God be not therefore a solver
    of riddles.
Rather look about you and you shall see Him playing
    with your children.
And look into space; you shall see Him walking
    in the cloud, outstretching His arms in the
    lightning and descending in rain.
You shall see Him smiling in flowers, then rising and
    waving His hands in trees.

Gibran critiques religion as a box, a thing, an identity where, like Blake,
he saw the institutions of the established church as getting in the way
of a true communion with God. Here are Gibran's views (recorded by
Mary Haskell) as quoted in *Kahlil Gibran: Man and Poet*:

Christianity has been very far from the teachings of Christ. In
the second or third century, people were not vigorous enough
to take the strong food that Christ gave; they ate only the
weak food in the Gospels, or what they thought they found
there and in the teaching of the men that came after Christ.
They could not face the gigantic self that Christ taught ... The
greatest teaching of Christ was the Kingdom of Heaven, and
that is within you.[*]

\*    Quoted in Bushrui and Jenkins 1998, p. 250.

He felt acutely the essential truth at the heart of all religions, and his desire for universal brotherhood, understanding and love, recognizing the unity of all faiths, is his central message:

> 'If we were to do away with the [non-essentials of the] various religions,' Gibran once proposed, 'we would find ourselves united and enjoying one great faith and religion, abounding in brotherhood.'[*]

As he wrote in *A Tear and a Smile*:

> You are my brother and I love you.
> I love you when you prostrate yourself in your mosque, and
>     kneel in your church, and pray in your synagogue,
> You and I are sons of one faith – the Spirit.[†]

---

[*]    Kahlil Gibran, 'Iram, City of Lofty Pillars', in *A Treasury of Kahlil Gibran* 1965, p. 135.
[†]    *A Tear and a Smile* (Gibran 1950), p. 168.

# On Death

Then Almitra spoke, saying, We would ask now of
    Death.
And he said:
You would know the secret of death.
But how shall you find it unless you seek it in the
    heart of life?
The owl whose night-bound eyes are blind unto the
    day cannot unveil the mystery of light.
If you would indeed behold the spirit of death,
    open your heart wide unto the body of
    life.
For life and death are one, even as the river and the
    sea are one.

In the depth of your hopes and desires lies your silent
    knowledge of the beyond;
And like seeds dreaming beneath the snow your heart
    dreams of spring.
Trust the dreams, for in them is hidden the gate to
    eternity.
Your fear of death is but the trembling of the
    shepherd when he stands before the king whose
    hand is to be laid upon him in honour.
Is the shepherd not joyful beneath his trembling, that
    he shall wear the mark of the king?
Yet is he not more mindful of his trembling?

For what is it to die but to stand naked in the wind
    and to melt into the sun?

And what is it to cease breathing, but to free the
breath from its restless tides, that it may rise and
expand and seek God unencumbered?

Only when you drink from the river of silence shall
you indeed sing.
And when you have reached the mountain top, then
you shall begin to climb.
And when the earth shall claim your limbs then shall
you truly dance.

On the subject of death Gibran has elsewhere written:

Death does not change us. It only frees that which is real in us
– our consciousness.[*]

The essence of being remains and is released fully into the universe;
'death changes nothing but the masks that cover our faces', as Gibran
was to write later in *The Garden of the Prophet*.[†] For him it was truly
as in Shakespeare's *The Tempest* simply to 'suffer a sea-change / Into
something rich and strange' and nothing to be feared. As Mikhail
Naimy recorded:

How often we have talked of Death – Gibran and I – and called
it the twin of Life – another birth.[‡]

[*]   Quoted in Bushrui and Jenkins 1998, p. 157.
[†]   *The Garden of the Prophet* (Gibran 1954), p. 47.
[‡]   Naimy 1967, p. 11.

# The Farewell

And now it was evening.

And Almitra the seeress said, Blessed be this
     day and this place and your spirit that has
     spoken.

And he answered, Was it I who spoke? Was I not also
     a listener?


Then he descended the steps of the Temple and all
     the people followed him. And he reached his
     ship and stood upon the deck.

And facing the people again, he raised his voice and
     said:

People of Orphalese, the wind bids me leave you.

Less hasty am I than the wind, yet I must go.

We wanderers, ever seeking the lonelier way, begin no
     day where we have ended another day; and no
     sunrise finds us where sunset left us.

Even while the earth sleeps we travel.

We are the seeds of the tenacious plant, and it is in
     our ripeness and our fullness of heart that we
     are given to the wind and are scattered.

Brief were my days among you, and briefer still the
     words I have spoken.

But should my voice fade in your ears, and my
     love vanish in your memory, then I will come
     again,

And with a richer heart and lips more yielding to the
     spirit will I speak.

Yea, I shall return with the tide,

And though death may hide me, and the greater
silence enfold me, yet again will I seek your
understanding.
And not in vain will I seek.
If aught I have said is truth, that truth shall reveal
itself in a clearer voice, and in words more kin to
your thoughts.

I go with the wind, people of Orphalese, but not
down into emptiness;
And if this day is not a fulfilment of your needs and
my love, then let it be a promise till another day.
Man's needs change, but not his love, nor his desire
that his love should satisfy his needs.
Know therefore, that from the greater silence I shall
return.
The mist that drifts away at dawn, leaving but dew in
the fields, shall rise and gather into a cloud and
then fall down in rain.
And not unlike the mist have I been.
In the stillness of the night I have walked in your
streets, and my spirit has entered your houses,
And your heart-beats were in my heart, and your
breath was upon my face, and I knew you all.
Ay, I knew your joy and your pain, and in your sleep
your dreams were my dreams.
And often times I was among you a lake among the
mountains.
I mirrored the summits in you and the bending
slopes, and ever the passing flocks of your
thoughts and your desires.
And to my silence came the laughter of your children in
streams, and the longing of your youths in rivers.
And when they reached my depth the streams and the
rivers ceased not yet to sing.

But sweeter still than laughter and greater than
    longing came to me.
It was the boundless in you;
The vast man in whom you are all but cells and
    sinews;
He in whose chant all your singing is but a soundless
    throbbing.
It is in the vast man that you are vast,
And in beholding him that I beheld you and loved
    you.
For what distances can love reach that are not in that
    vast sphere?
What visions, what expectations and what
    presumptions can outsoar that flight?
Like a giant oak tree covered with apple blossoms is
    the vast man in you.
His might binds you to the earth, his fragrance lifts you
    into space, and in his durability you are deathless.

You have been told that, even like a chain, you are as
    weak as your weakest link.
This is but half a truth. You are also as strong as your
    strongest link.
To measure you by your smallest deed is to reckon
    the power of ocean by the frailty of its foam.
To judge you by your failures is to cast blame upon
    the seasons for their inconstancy.

Ay, you are like an ocean,
And though heavy-grounded ships await the tide
    upon your shores, yet, even like an ocean, you
    cannot hasten your tides.
And like the seasons you are also,
And though in your winter you deny your spring.
Yet spring, reposing within you, smiles in her
    drowsiness and is not offended.

Think not I say these things in order that you may
say the one to the other, 'He praises us well. He
saw but the good in us.'
I only speak to you in words of that which you
yourselves know in thought.
And what is word knowledge but a shadow of
wordless knowledge?
Your thoughts and my words are waves from a sealed
memory that keeps records of our yesterdays,
And of the ancient days when the earth knew not us
nor herself,
And of nights when earth was upwrought with
confusion.

Wise men have come to you to give you of their
wisdom. I came to take of your wisdom:
And behold I have found that which is greater than
wisdom.
It is the flame spirit in you ever gathering more of
itself,
While you, heedless of its expansion, bewail the
withering of your days.
It is life in quest of life in bodies that fear the grave.

There are no graves here.
These mountains and plains are a cradle and a
stepping-stone.
Whenever you pass by the field where you have laid
your ancestors look well thereupon, and you
shall see yourselves and your children dancing
hand in hand.
Verily you often make merry without knowing.

Others have come to you to whom for golden
promises made unto your faith you have given
but riches and power and glory.

Less than a promise have I given, and yet more
    generous have you been to me.
You have given me my deeper thirsting after life.
Surely there is no greater gift to a man than that
    which turns all his aims into parching lips and
    all life into a fountain.
And in this lies my honour and my reward, –
That whenever I come to the fountain to drink I find
    the living water itself thirsty;
And it drinks me while I drink it.

Some of you have deemed me proud and over-shy to
    receive gifts.
Too proud indeed am I to receive wages, but not
    gifts. And though I have eaten my berries among
    the hills when you would have had me sit at your
    board,
And slept in the portico of the temple when you
    would gladly have sheltered me,
Yet was it not your loving mindfulness of my days
    and my nights that made food sweet to my
    mouth and girdled my sleep with visions?

For this I bless you most:
You give much and know not that you give at all.
Verily the kindness that gazes upon itself in a mirror
    turns to stone,
And a good deed that calls itself by tender names
    becomes the parent to a curse.

And some of you have called me aloof, and drunk
    with my own aloneness,
And you have said, 'He holds council with the trees
    of the forest, but not with men.
He sits alone on hill-tops and looks down upon our
    city.'

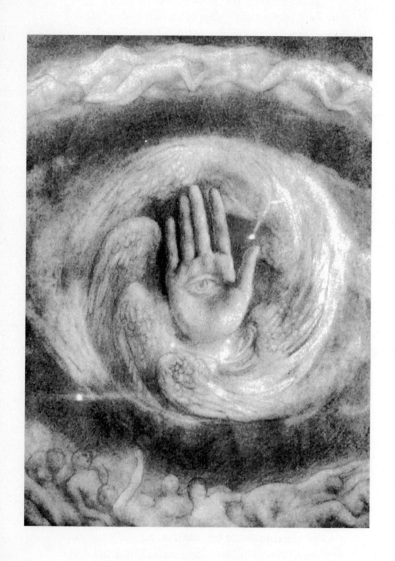

True it is that I have climbed the hills and walked in
　　　remote places.
How could I have seen you save from a great height
　　　or a great distance?
How can one be indeed near unless he be far?

And others among you called unto me, not in words,
　　　and they said,
'Stranger, stranger, lover of unreachable heights, why
　　　dwell you among the summits where the eagles
　　　build their nests?
Why seek you the unattainable?
What storms would you trap in your net,
And what vaporous birds do you hunt in the sky?
Come and be one of us.
Descend and appease your hunger with our bread
　　　and quench your thirst with our wine.'
In the solitude of their souls they said these things;
But were their solitude deeper they would have
　　　known that I sought but the secret of your joy
　　　and your pain,
And I hunted only your larger selves that walk the sky.

But the hunter was also the hunted;
For many of my arrows left my bow only to seek my
　　　own breast.
And the flier was also the creeper;
For when my wings were spread in the sun their
　　　shadow upon the earth was also a turtle.
And I the believer was also the doubter;
For often have I put my finger in my own wound that
　　　I might have the greater belief in you and the
　　　greater knowledge of you.

And it is with this belief and this knowledge that I
　　　say,

You are not enclosed within your bodies, nor
    confined to houses of fields.
That which is you dwells above the mountain and
    roves with the wind.
It is not a thing that crawls into the sun for warmth
    or digs holes into darkness for safety,
But a thing free, a spirit that envelops the earth and
    moves in the ether.

If these be vague words, then seek not to clear them.
Vague and nebulous is the beginning of all things,
    but not their end,
And I fain would have you remember me as a
    beginning.
Life and all that lives, is conceived in the mist and not
    in the crystal.
And who knows but a crystal is mist in decay?

This would I have you remember in remembering me:
That which seems most feeble and bewildered in you
    is the strongest and most determined.
Is it not your breath that has erected and hardened
    the structure of your bones?
And is it not a dream which none of your remember
    having dreamt, that builded your city and
    fashioned all there is in it?
Could you but see the tides of that breath you would
    cease to see all else,
And if you could hear the whispering of the dream
    you would hear no other sound.

But you do not see, nor do you hear, and it is well.
The veil that clouds your eyes shall be lifted by the
    hands that wove it,
And the clay that fills your ears shall be pierced by
    those finders that kneaded it. And you shall see

And you shall hear.
Yet you shall not deplore having known blindness,
    nor regret having been deaf.
For in that day you shall know the hidden purposes
    in all things,
And you shall bless darkness as you would bless light.

After saying these things he looked about him, and
    he saw the pilot of his ship standing by the helm
    and gazing now at the full sails and now at the
    distance.
And he said:
Patient, over-patient, is the captain of my ship.
The wind blows, and restless are the sails;
Even the rudder begs direction;
Yet quietly my captain awaits my silence.
And these my mariners, who have heard the choir of
    the greater sea, they too have heard me patiently.
Now they shall wait no longer.
I am ready.
The stream has reached the sea, and once more the
    great mother holds her son against her breast.

Fare you well, people of Orphalese.
This day has ended.
It is closing upon us even as the water-lily upon its
    own tomorrow.
What was given us here we shall keep,
And if it suffices not, then again we must come
    together and together stretch our hands unto the
    giver.
Forget not that I shall come back to you.
A little while, and my longing shall gather dust and
    foam for another body.
A little while, a moment of rest upon the wind, and
    another woman shall bear me.

Farewell to you and the youth I have spent with you.
It was but yesterday we met in a dream.
You have sung to me in my aloneness, and I of your
longings have built a tower in the sky.
But now our sleep has fled and our dream is over, and
it is no longer dawn.
The noontide is upon us and our half waking has
turned to fuller day, and we must part.
If in the twilight of memory we should meet once
more, we shall speak once again together and
you shall sing to me a deeper song.
And if our hands should meet in another dream we
shall build another tower in the sky.

So saying he made a signal to the seamen, and
straightway they weighed anchor and cast the
ship loose from its moorings, and they moved
eastward.
And a cry came from the people as a single heart,
and it rose into the dusk and was carried out
over the sea like a great trumpeting.
Only Almitra was silent, gazing after the ship until it
had vanished into the mist.
And when all the people were dispersed she still
stood alone upon the sea-wall, remembering in
her heart his saying,

'A little while, a moment of rest upon the wind and
another woman shall bear me.'

As befits the ending of such a work, the final section is filled with
beautiful allusions and symbolism. While the 'greater silence' talks of

death, the 'mist' refers to mystery and eternity, although commonly representing the condition of error and confusion. Gibran's letters to May Ziadah are full of references to mist, for example:

> Which one of us is capable of transforming the gentle mist into statues or sculptured form.[*]
>
> I am mist that cloaks things but never unites them, I am mist unchanged into rain water. I am mist, and mist is my loneliness and my being alone ... My misfortune, however, is that this mist is my reality, and that it longs to meet with another mist in the sky.[†]
>
> I work in the mist, meet people in the mist, even sleep, dream and wake up in the mist ... It is a divine trace ... which brings near that which is remote, uncovers that which is hidden, and illuminates all things ... I aver that all we say, do or think is worthless when compared to a single moment spent in the mist.[‡]

The 'vast man' could be viewed as a reference to the universe or cosmos as being wrapped up within the human soul, as expressed by the Súfí saying 'the universe is a vast man and man is a small universe'. Similarly, the 'giant oak tree covered with apple blossoms' is God. The many symbolic uses of the oak tree include that of Christ as strength in adversity; in Hebrew tradition the oak is the emblem of the Divine Presence. 'Fountain' speaks of fertility and giving, while 'hills' are the dimensions of thought and inspiration.

The phrase 'put my finger in my own wound' is a reference to Jesus' disciple Thomas Didymus (known as 'Doubting Thomas') who, when told of the reappearance of Christ, stated 'except I shall see in his hands the print of the nails, and put my finger into the print of the nails, and thrust my hand into his side, I will not believe'.[§]

Finally, 'crystal' stands for clarity. In the Buddhist tradition, crystal symbolizes pure mind or perfect insight; in Christianity the crystal ball denoted the world of the light of God. Crystal is commonly associated with purity, spiritual perfection and knowledge. 'Tower in the sky' refers to hope for a future of spiritual fulfilment, while 'dream' refers to life on earth.

---

[*]   Bushrui and al-Kuzbari 1995, p. 8.

[†]   *Ibid.*, p. 39.

[‡]   *Ibid.*, p. 46.

[§]   John 20:24–25. See also Bushrui and al-Kuzbari 1995, pp. 69–70.

# Bibliography

*A Treasury of Kahlil Gibran*, ed. M. Wolf, translated from the
Arabic by Anthony Rizcallah Ferris (New York: Citadel
Press, 1965).

Alfred, Lord Tennyson, *The Major Works*, ed. Adam Roberts
(New York: Oxford University Press, 2009).

Arberry, A.J., *Súfism* (London: George Allen & Unwin, 1950).

Bushrui, Suheil, and Munro, John, eds., *Kahlil Gibran: Essays
and Introductions* (Beirut: Rihani House, 1970).

Bushrui, Suheil, *Kahlil Gibran of Lebanon* (Buckinghamshire:
Colin Smythe, 1989).

Bushrui, Suheil, and Jenkins, Joe, *Kahlil Gibran: Man and
Poet* (Oxford and Boston: Oneworld Publications, 1998).

Bushrui, Suheil, and Gotch, Paul, comp. and ed., *Gibran of
Lebanon* (Beirut: Librairie du Liban, 1975).

Bushrui, Suheil, and al-Kuzbari, Salma H., ed. and trans.,
*Gibran: Love Letters* (Oxford: Oneworld Publications,
1995).

Bushrui, Suheil, 'Kahlil Gibran: Poet of Ecology.' *Resurgence*
May/June 1996.

*The Collected Works of Oscar Wilde* (Hertfordshire:
Wordsworth Editions Limited, 2007).

*The Complete Poetry & Prose of William Blake*, ed. David V.
Erdman (New York: Anchor Books, 1988).

*The Complete Writings of William Blake with All the Variant
Readings*, ed. Geoffrey Keynes (London and New York:
Oxford University Press, 1957).

El-Hage, George Nicolas, 'William Blake and Kahlil Gibran: Poets of Prophetic Vision.' Dissertation, State University of New York (Binghamton: El-Hage, 1980).

Gail, Marziah, *Other People, Other Places* (Oxford: George Ronald, 1982).

Gibran, Kahlil, *Spirits Rebellious*, translated from the Arabic by Anthony R. Ferris (New York: Philosophical Library, 1947).

Gibran, Kahlil, *A Tear and a Smile*, translated from the Arabic by H.M. Nahmad (London: Heinemann, 1950).

Gibran, Kahlil, *The Garden of the Prophet* (London: Heinemann, 1954).

Gibran, Kahlil, *Sand and Foam* (London: Heinemann, 1954).

Gibran, Kahlil, *The Voice of the Master*, translated from the Arabic by Anthony R. Ferris (New York: Citadel Press, 1958).

Gibran, Kahlil, *Thoughts and Meditations*, ed. and translated from the Arabic by Anthony R. Ferris (New York: Citadel Press, 1960).

Gibran, Kahlil, *Mirrors of the Soul*, translated from the Arabic by Joseph Sheban (New York: Philosophical Library, 1965).

Gibran, Kahlil, *The Prophet*, introduced and annotated by Suheil Bushrui (Oxford: Oneworld Publications, 1995).

Gibran, Kahlil, *The Treasured Writings of Kahlil Gibran*, ed. Anthony R. Ferris, Martin L. Wolf and Andrew Dib Sherfan (New York: Castle Books, 2010).

Hawi, Khalil S., *Kahlil Gibran: His Background, Character and Works* (Beirut: American University of Beirut, 1963).

Hilu, Virginia, comp. and ed., *Beloved Prophet: the Love Letters of Kahlil Gibran and Mary Haskell and her Private Journal* (London: Alfred Knopf, 1972).

Hilu, Virginia, comp. and ed., *Beloved Prophet: the Love Letters of Kahlil Gibran and Mary Haskell and her Private Journal* (London: Quartet Books, 1973).

*The Holy Bible*, King James Version (Grand Rapids: Zondervan, 2002).

Honnol, Annamarie, comp. and ed., *Vignettes from the Life of 'Abdu'l-Bahá* (Oxford: George Ronald, 1982).

Huwayik, Yusef, *Gibran in Paris* (New York: Popular Library, 1976).

Ibish, Yusuf, 'Ibn Arabi's Theory of Journeying', in *Contemplation and Action in World Religions*, ed. Y. Ibish and I. Marculescu (Seattle and London: University of Washington Press, 1977–8).

Naimy, Mikhail, *Kahlil Gibran: His Life and His Works* (Beirut: Khayats, 1967).

Orfalea, G. and Elmusa, S., eds., *Grape Leaves: A Century of Arab American*, translated by Andrew Ghareeb (Salt Lake City: University of Utah Press, 1988).

Otto, Annie S., *The Parables of Kahlil Gibran: An Interpretation of His Writings and His Art* (New York: Citadel Press, 1963).

Pickthall, Marmaduke, *The Meaning of the Glorious Qur'án* (London: al-Furqan Publications, undated).

*The Poems of William Blake*, ed. W.H. Stevenson, text by David V. Erdman (London: Longman, 1971).

Quiller-Couch, Sir Arthur Thomas, *The Oxford Book of English Verse* (Oxford: Clarendon, 1919).

Reynolds, Susan, 'Kahlil Gibran and 'Abdu'l-Bahá', presented at the Second International Conference on Kahlil Gibran (May 2012).

Rihani, Ameen, *The Book of Khalid* (New York: Dodd, Mead & Co., 1911).

Shehadi, William, *Kahlil Gibran: a Prophet in the Making* (Beirut: American University of Beirut, 1991).